Praise for SYSTEMology

"*SYSTEMology* is a must for any business owner and their leadership team. It provides a powerful, practical, and simple way for systemising your business."

GINO WICKMAN – author of *Traction and Entrepreneurial Leap*

"David Jenyns, in his book *SYSTEMology*, provides every business owner the recipe to building their business playbook. What Michael Gerber started, David Jenyns completed."

JACK DALY – author of *Hyper Sales Growth*

"My unequivocal recommendation is that every entrepreneur and business owner must have this outstanding workbook... and implement it!"

KERRY BOULTON – CEO and Founder, The Exit Strategy Group

"This book is going to be a category killer, I am certain of it. I have read many books on business systems and nothing else comes close."

ALLAN DIB – author of *The 1-Page Marketing Plan*

"David provides an invaluable framework that will add enormous value to any business owner wise enough to embrace it. Smart, current and immensely valuable. Simple as that."

ANDREW GRIFFITHS – author of *The Big Book of Small Business*

"Many books have workflows you can follow, but this one teaches you how to systemise your business without all the stress (and crazy time commitment) most business owners experience when trying to grow."

RHAMY ALEJEAL – author of *People Processes*

"This book by David Jenyns is the new standard for building systems."

DALE BEAUMONT – CEO and Founder, Business Blueprint

"I'd suggest dropping everything to read and apply the learnings from David's book."

"This is a great piece of work with a profound level of insight and experience behind it that is easy to miss because of the simplicity of the writing."

"This book provides real value to business owners, helping them to work less and be happier."

"David Jenyns provides a clear, easy to follow system for creating systems in your business. The best part: you will discover that it does not have to be YOU creating the systems."

"For someone who has taught and preached the value of systems for 16 years, this book is the simplest, yet most effective book I have EVER read to help any and every business owner ready to systemise their business!"

"Pick it up. Do it. Change your business and your life. Simple as that."

"Immensely practical. Immensely valuable. And immensely important."

"I have been systemising businesses now for over 20 years, and this is the book I wish I'd read 20 years ago! David's system is so brilliantly simple that *SYSTEMology* will be on the essential reading list for my clients moving forward."

"If you're a founder or CEO – and you want your business to run like a well oiled machine – the pittance you'll invest in a copy of his book will pay you back hundreds and thousands of times. I highly recommend it."

ALEXI NEOCLEOUS – CEO and Founder, Fubbi

"*SYSTEMology* will make your business more valuable and help you get your life back – a thorough framework for moving out of survival mode in your business and systemising it to scale and ultimately be saleable without your day to day involvement."

GREG CASSAR – Marketing Director, MarketingBoost

"*SYSTEMology* is the answer to the colossal failure rates of small businesses worldwide. The strategy and tactics the book details offer a pathway to take command of each crucial facet of any business."

PETER CARRUTHERS – author of *CrashProof your Business*

"*SYSTEMology* is, hands down, the most practical process for creating systems. David makes it fun and simple to follow (and this is coming from someone who isn't a natural systems guy, but more of a hustler)."

JOE FIER – Host of the *Hustle and Flowchart* Podcast

"Implementing the *SYSTEMology* structured approach across our companies has had a tremendous impact on our teams productivity and has improved operations throughout the group. A must read for every leader looking to grow."

PETE WILLIAMS – author of *Cadence: a tale of fast business growth*

"The 7-stage process outlined, if followed, will change your business, give you back your life and add multiples to the sale value if you plan to exit. Read it, implement it, then watch the magic happen."

ADAM HOULAHAN – Founder, Prominence Global

Editing by	Kelsey Garlick
Cover Design by	July Amarillo
Interior Layout by	Olivier Darbonville
Publishing Consultant	Linda Diggle

A catalogue record for this book is available from the National Library of Australia

SYSTEMology

Create time, reduce errors and scale your profits with proven business systems

DAVID JENYNS

SYSTEMology

[sis-tuhm-ol-uh-jee] *noun*

The step-by-step system for systemising any business and removing key person dependency.

Contents

Foreword

From the desk of:

Michael E. Gerber, author of the E-Myth Books.

IT DIDN'T TAKE MUCH TO CONVINCE ME to write the Foreword to David Jenyns new book, SYSTEMology.

Indeed, all he had to do was ask.

Because David and I go back a ways, digging deep into each other's work, passion, and, most important, his integrity.

David is a trustworthy man.

Why is that important?

Because David is also a systems thinker, a creator of the first order, an entrepreneur who has done what I write about, not once, but several times.

Creating small companies, going to work on those small companies, systemising those small companies to prepare them to grow but, and here's the most important thing about all this, to grow without David having to remain the "chief cook and bottle washer" responsible for every little wrinkle and widget, every single decision waiting desperately to be made.

No, David, built SYSTEMology into every single one of his new ventures from the get-go.

And that's why this book is so essential for you.

Because in this book, David explains, step by step by step by step, exactly how you can do the very same thing.

In short, David has built a SYSTEM out of SYSTEMology to make it literally impossible for a small growing entrepreneur like you to make the mistakes almost every small business owner is doomed to make... creating a business that's totally dependent upon them.

Which is really all I have to say about it.

I invented "working ON your business, instead of IN it" almost 43 years ago with my very first E-Myth Book.

And here I am telling you that David Jenyns has not only DONE it, but he's now written the brilliant book to teach you exactly how to do it, too!

Read it.

Relish it.

But most important, DO it!

It's the magical elixir for what ails you!

Michael E. Gerber
Author of the E-Myth Books
The E-Myth Founder

Introduction

IMAGINE FOR A MOMENT THAT the number one thought leader in your industry (the Oprah, if you will) calls you out of the blue and asks you to join them, right away, on a dream project for three months.

Could you do it? Could your business survive without you for that long? Could you risk downing tools and jumping on board the opportunity of a lifetime?

And could you have taken it on like an apprenticeship, with no pay?

A little over three years ago, I had an experience so strange that I knew it HAD to be real. The kind of scenario where I knew that not even the oddest, late night cheese-and-pickle sandwich-inspired fever dream could conjure up what was currently happening.

It was 7 am and I was looking at an email I'd received from someone called Luz Delia Gerber. I didn't recognise the full name, but I was familiar with a certain Michael E. Gerber, author of the E-Myth series of books, the original of which is generally said to be one of the best-selling business books of all time.

I figured it was just a coincidence. I'd never met Michael E. Gerber, and I had no relationship with anyone who knew him. But I had to know …

All the email said was, "Call me," so that's what I did. It was an American phone number and I knew it was afternoon on the west coast, so it didn't matter that it was still early morning in Melbourne, Australia.

As it happens, the Gerbers like to record their calls, so I have the transcript of the conversation. What follows isn't paraphrased or edited. It's verbatim.

David: "Good morning. This is David Jenyns, just calling from Australia. I'm actually after Luz – I think it is."

Luz Delia: "Oh my God, is this the real David?"

David: "This is the real David. How are you?"

Luz Delia: "Oh, I am fine. I did want to cry just because … You have no idea what you picking up the phone and calling me is doing to life – yours and mine."

David: "Okay, that's a good thing. Yes. I know your message came through late last night. I don't know if you know but I'm based in Australia. So that's why um, yeah."

Luz Delia: "Yeah. Okay, that's it. I just finished watching your videos."

Dave: "Fantastic!"

Luz Delia: "I just watched one and was just now looking for it because I wanted to send it to my husband because I've been on a journey this morning. I mean, I'll tell you how I met you and how I found you and but it's all spiritual. It's all part of the journey I'm on. Anyway, I just knew that I had to talk to you. I just had to have a conversation with you. Well, and then I dared to say 'call me now.'

"I'll go to wherever you are. Come here. I need you, I have to talk to you. I just have to get over the shock."

David: "What a great way to start my day."

Luz Delia: "Do you know Michael E. Gerber? Do you know the name? Do you know his work?"

If you're getting the sense that I was a little stunned by all of this, you're reading it correctly. It was surreal. And not just because Luz Delia was talking as if I was the universe's gift to her.

I was – and still am – a huge fan of Michael E. Gerber and his work. If you've read any of his books, particularly in the E-Myth series, you'll probably know why. If you've yet to have the privilege, I urge you to do so (after you've finished this book, of course).

Gerber is a legend. You know the popular business adage, "Don't work IN your business. Work ON your business"? He came up with that. He's inspired millions of business owners around the world.

And now I was speaking to his wife, and she was talking to me as if I was the answer to some cosmic prayer.

Luz Delia and I had a very long conversation, but the bottom line was that Gerber, at the age of eighty, was getting ready to launch book number twenty-nine, and the final work in the E-Myth series. For the first time, he wanted to self-publish (the previous books were published by HarperCollins), and he wanted someone to show him how to do it.

Having followed the successful launch of my previous book, *Authority Content*, Luz Delia had decided that I was the person to head up the project.

There was just one snag …

It was going to take sixty-plus hours of work per week, for a period of about twelve weeks. For three months I was going to have to eat, sleep and breathe *The E-Myth*. Which meant that all my own personal projects and business responsibilities would have to be put on hold. Oh, and did I mention I volunteered to do the job unpaid?

What would you have done if you'd been in my shoes?

If Gerber had approached me two years before he did, I would have had to decline the opportunity. Two years ago, there wasn't a chance that I could just walk away from my business for that long. I was too enmeshed in the day-to-day operations. Without me, there was no business, and I'd have been risking not just my livelihood, but that of all my employees.

Ironically, for all my appreciation of Gerber's work, I was doing exactly what he advised against. Working IN my business, rather than ON my business.

Fortunately, it wasn't two years ago. This opportunity came along after I'd discovered and developed SYSTEMology, and I knew for a fact that without me around …

My business was going to be just fine.

SYSTEMology was handling my business with such efficiency, I knew that I could leave it for three months and it would barely notice my absence. If anything, it would run smoother without me looking over everyone's shoulders.

I worked on Gerber's project for three months. I wrote thousands of emails, made hundreds of phone calls and lined up more interviews than you can poke a stick at. It was hard work, but it was simultaneously one of the easiest projects I've ever been involved in simply because I had only to mention Gerber's name and people would fall over themselves in their eagerness to be involved.

The short version of the story was that Gerber's twenty-ninth book became his first to be ranked as an Amazon Best Seller within twenty-four hours of its launch. To celebrate, Michael invited me and a few friends who had helped out with the launch to attend one of his last events, called the Dreaming Room, in Carlsbad, California. I was then invited to stay on to facilitate a mastermind group dedicated to the future legacy of Michael's work.

To top it all off, the Gerbers asked me if I'd consider running their business!

I wasn't expecting that! I literally hadn't had any connection to the Gerbers four months earlier, and here I was now being offered the company. I declined – with some difficulty – not because it wasn't a great offer but because I am on my own path now. That, and there's no chance my wife would move to America, away from her family.

Looking back now, this experience was nothing short of magical. And while there are probably a hundred lessons I could share with you, I wanted to draw your attention to one in particular.

Serendipity happens in business all the time. When Luz Delia contacted me, she did so because of the work I'd done in my previous business (my digital agency, which you'll learn more about later). She had no idea that I was also working on SYSTEMology and how it would align so perfectly with the Gerber legacy.

The fact is, business and life are non-linear – that is, things don't always happen in a logical order or a straight line. There is a level of randomness that can not be easily explained.

Oh, we act as if it's a linear thing. We read books about success and seek to learn the secrets of how to be the greatest at this or the master of that. But knowledge only gets you so far. Success stories, for the most part, are just that: stories – narratives that people construct to try to explain why things turned out the way they did, by stripping out all the things that didn't work. The implication is that if someone follows the same journey, minus the dead ends, missteps and failures, rapid success is all but guaranteed. In reality, everyone's journey to success, no matter how much they might try to follow someone else's model, is unique, convoluted and, to a certain extent, random.

Anything but linear.

Sometimes you'll get up one morning and you'll have an email from a personal hero inviting you to come and work with them because you did

X, Y and Z and their wife just happened to spot something you put out into the world.

Opportunities rarely come at the end of a steady upwards curve. Success is lumpy and opportunity knocks when you're least expecting it.

Sure, you can lay the foundations, work hard and prepare yourself. But your most significant opportunities won't be willed into existence by simple visualisation or by following a special formula. They're going to happen when they're going to happen and the only thing – the ONLY thing – over which you have any control is whether you're ready and available to seize them.

What opportunities have you missed?

Think about this for a minute.

Not too hard because it might depress you, but think about it.

How many opportunities have already passed you by because you were too swamped with the heaving mass of work that your business throws at you every day?

I'm not just talking about having to turn down opportunities because you're too busy. I'm talking about opportunities that you didn't even notice because you barely have time to scoff down a lunchtime sandwich, let alone rise above the noise, study the big picture and spot the big breaks that are in your periphery.

That's where I was a few years ago, and if I hadn't found the motivation to change my chaotic existence, I would have had to tell Luz Delia and Michael E. Gerber that I simply wasn't available.

Just the thought of that makes me feel sad.

Now, I'm not sure where your headspace is at this moment. Maybe you're early in your career and you're looking to ramp things up – to make your business more efficient and build it for scale. Maybe you're getting older and want to reduce your working hours to improve your health. Or perhaps you just want to spend more time with your friends and family.

Or maybe you're wanting to open up a world of new, exciting opportunities?

Whatever your reasons for picking up this book, understand that the primary purpose of SYSTEMology is to create space for the business owner – to systemise the business to the point where you can step away from the day-to-day operations and know with confidence that your business will continue to perform to your standards.

You might have no desire to reduce your hundred-hour work week. And you don't have to. But the reality is that most business owners have crazy, working-their-fingers-to-the-bone schedules, not because they WANT to but because they HAVE to. They have no other option other than letting the business fall apart.

SYSTEMology gives you the freedom to choose. You should be able to have a choice in how you run your business. In it. Out of it. Ten hours a week. A hundred hours a week. Instead of the business forcing you to conform to its will, you should be able to shape your business to conform to your will.

It will take time and effort and challenge many of your strongest beliefs about business, but trust me, it will be worth it.

All your hard work, persistence, talent and creativity will pay off eventually. It's just impossible to predict when those magical moments are going to strike. The fact is, all the best ideas, the biggest breakthroughs and the most tremendous opportunities come when the business owner creates space.

But you must learn to engineer this space. Systems hold the key.

Is this the right book for you?

This book isn't about getting the right mindset.

It will not help you create your company purpose, vision or mission. It won't help you define your values, set your goals or create a business plan.

It won't help you identify your target audience, their problems or how to get that product/market fit.

If you haven't yet addressed these foundations of business, it's best you do that BEFORE you continue reading this book. The good news is, there are already plenty of great books that address these topics.

This book aims to solve a different problem. One that presents itself a little further down the line when building your business.

This problem arises AFTER the business owner lays a good foundation and has achieved some level of traction. They have built a reputation for delivering great products and services and this earns them repeat and referral business. The business has good cash flow, and from the outside looking in they look like a huge success. But the hidden reality is that they work extremely long hours to keep their business functioning.

The problem is, most small business owners can't afford to step away from their business for more than a day or two. They've built a machine that depends upon them and now they're stuck. Worse still, this is the inverse to what they were looking to achieve when they started in business – and it's a serious problem.

Unfortunately, what makes this such a hard problem to solve is that the solution lives in their blind spot. Typically, business owners are big-picture people – they're quick-thinking problem-solvers who focus on solving the most urgent problems. And while these skills are great when the business is in start-up mode, the strengthening of these abilities often becomes the primary reason for not making it to the next level of business growth.

If this sounds like you, you've reached the bridge that all business owners must cross but the majority don't.

You must learn to clone yourself and your best team members so that the business can grow without single-person dependency. You must evolve from being an employee of a business you own to a TRUE business owner – the owner of a profitable enterprise that works without you.

The solution to the problem lives in the development of your business systems. That is, the non-urgent but extremely important, detail-oriented task of documenting, organising and optimising how your business functions.

Rarely do business owners get excited by the idea of documenting their systems ... but having a business that works without your constant oversight? That's a different story.

Perhaps you've read books like *The E-Myth*, *Traction*, *Scaling Up* and *Built to Sell*, and you're already sold on the idea of creating systems. But like most busy business owners, you've either never really gotten around to it or you've tried to systemise your business in the past and failed.

So, where is the solution for you and your small business?

You might have read about Six Sigma and tried to apply it to your business but found there was too much bureaucracy and rigidity in the methodology. Maybe you have realised the Lean methodology was developed for mass production facilities and doesn't suit your small business. Maybe you looked into ISO accreditation and realised it's more about ticking boxes to say you have systems within your business than having your team actually use them. You're not alone – to date, much of the work developed around the topic of business systems has been geared towards larger businesses.

This sets small businesses up to fail right from the start because the methodologies simply weren't designed for their size. They're complicated, costly, time-consuming, and the team doesn't follow them anyway. Small business is a different beast. There's little margin for error and no room for doing activities that don't dramatically impact the bottom line.

The good news is, this book contains the solution. It's a revolutionary *new* approach to business systemisation. It is, quite literally, the system for systemising your business.

Of course, if you're not the business owner, that's perfectly fine too. There's a good chance you work with one and someone you know has passed this book along to you. If so, I'm excited for you too since, although you may not realise it just yet, you're going to play a very important role in transforming the business you work in.

At what stage is your business in terms of systemisation?

To start, it's important to know where you are and where you're going. It sounds obvious, but with a clear understanding you're much more likely to reach the destination.

Is your business's intellectual property (IP) trapped in the brains of your best team members? Are you super dependent on these few key team members? Are the rest of your team making things up as they go? Do you have any documented systems? And if you do, does your team follow your systems or do you find yourself constantly reminding your team to follow them?

Having worked with hundreds of companies over the years, I have found companies typically find themselves in one of four stages: #1 Survival; #2 Stationary; #3 Scalable; #4 Saleable.

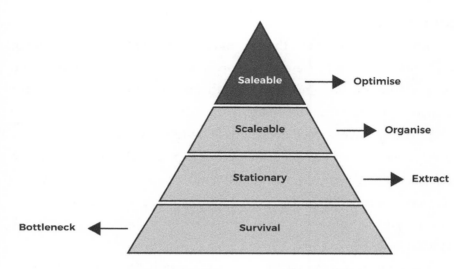

The four stages of business systemisation.

Stage #1: Survival

At the base of the pyramid, survival mode is where most business owners start. The business owner is in an endless loop of chasing the work, getting the work and doing the work. This creates up and down performance with lumpy results.

You're still figuring out product/market fit, you spend 80 per cent of your time in problem-solving mode and you're hustling your way through.

You've got one million ideas but the ability to execute on only a handful of things at any one time. This means you're trying lots of new things but you never really take anything to completion.

Your team (if you have one) makes things up as they go. It's not clear who is doing what and when tasks are due. There are no systems or processes, and no one really likes them anyway.

In short, this isn't a great state to remain in.

The business owner is quite often the bottleneck in this stage, and there's no real insight that systems are the 'way' and that they (the business owner) are not the best person to develop them – more on this later.

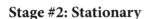

Stage #2: Stationary

In the stationary stage, the ups and downs have been smoothed out and you're starting to see a little more consistency in the business. You have a loose way of doing things, but this is still typically trapped in the heads of your best team members.

You may have a few documented systems but they're more like unorganised notes scattered all over the place. This lack of system certainty makes your business team-member dependent. You don't have the right tools or software, so the performance of the small number of systems you do have is average at best. This lack of clarity results in a lack of team 'buy-in'.

It often feels like the business owner is simply spinning plates. They create a to-do list for one team member and move onto the next. One after the other, the business owner lists out what needs to be done. Once they're all the way through the team, they have to circle back around to the first team member because it's time to assign out new tasks. This cycle never ends, and the business owner often feels like they run an adult daycare centre. Not to mention, the business owner rarely finds the time to do their own work!

Obviously, this still isn't a great place to be since your business often feels stationary. You've reached capacity and you can't seem to break through to that next level of business. To move beyond this stage, the secret is to extract and document your core systems.

Stage #3: Scalable

Once you've got a good amount of your core business systems documented, this is where things start to get interesting. You have now proven your core business model works. You still need to extract and organise systems from all business departments, but you're well on your way.

System performance has improved dramatically, and you're shifting the culture within your business. Your tools are clunky, and you still have to constantly remind your team to follow your process, but you've overcome any initial resistance.

Now is the time to focus on increasing your business capacity by installing human resources systems, finance systems and management systems. You also need to develop the ability to solve business problems well before they develop into more serious problems.

A funny thing happens at this stage. People often reach this point and think things are 'good enough'. They buy into the thought that *We're doing okay, we have most of our systems documented, we're a systemised business.*

The truth is, 'good enough' traps you. You don't want to stop here! The biggest wins and opportunities present themselves when you move to the final stage. You want to move your team's thinking from *We have to follow process* to *This is how we do things here*. Achieve this and the magic happens.

Stage #4: Saleable

The ultimate goal within business is to have a saleable asset – to have a business someone else would want to buy.

Don't get me wrong, whether you sell or not is your choice, but when your business is saleable you operate at a different level. You recognise your business as a collection of interdependent systems that can be engineered to deliver extraordinary outcomes. In this stage, you will have a clear 'way' of doing business, your operations run with the precision of a Swiss watch and your team upholds your systems-centred company culture.

No longer are you dependent on specific team members for things to work. The *systems* work and the people work the system. This is a different level of business, where you're able to rise above the noise and be deliberate and strategic in the work you do. You can begin to optimise your performance.

Once you reach this stage, systems become your competitive advantage and you'll look for constant and never-ending improvement. At this level you achieve what we call 'complete business reliability'.

Which stage are you in?

There is no 'right' or 'wrong' here, it just is what it is. Typically, most people who pick up this book are in the stationary stage with one foot in the survival stage, but let's think about you and where you are. Does one of the stages jump out at you, and what does it feel like to be in that stage?

Think about where you are and where you'd like to get to. It should be everyone's goal to move their business into the saleable stage – I mean, who wouldn't want complete business reliability? Just imagine what that will feel like when you reach that goal. What would it mean to you – to your business, to your family and your life?

This book provides a proven step-by-step blueprint for moving from Survival to Saleable.

"Yeah, but my business is different..."

A quick heads-up, though: no matter how effective SYSTEMology becomes, no matter how many businesses we revolutionise, or how many raving fans we create, it's natural to wonder *Will this work for me?* Maybe you're thinking about it right now. This is normal.

There's an old and rather depressing anecdote about a fully grown elephant held in place by a tiny stake in the ground. The elephant, if she chooses to, can escape with minimal effort; the only reason she doesn't is because that same slender stake was used to hold her in place when she was just a calf. She tugged and tugged on it when she was young and just a few feet high, but experience taught her to give up.

The elephant doesn't remain in captivity because it's incapable. It remains in captivity because previous attempts discouraged it. It has learned helplessness.

The truth is, this happens to all of us.

So, what are the 'stakes' that hold you back in business?

- Have you tried to systemise in the past but failed?
- Are you worried systems and processes will remove the creativity within your business?
- Do you think you need to be the one to create systems in your business?
- Do you believe systemisation is too time-consuming?
- Do you suspect that, even if you put systems in place, your team won't follow them?
- Do you believe you need to systemise with the efficiency of McDonald's?

These are all reasonable concerns, but don't let previous failed attempts fool you into thinking systemisation won't work for you. I believed many of these myths too, and it wasn't until I challenged my thinking that I discovered these ideas often stemmed from outdated information – methods designed for large corporate businesses or ideas shared by 'gurus' who don't practice what they preach.

Trust me, as you go through the SYSTEMology process, you'll begin to test these assumptions, bust the myths, and reach your own conclusions.

One final word before we begin. And that word is...

PATIENCE!

What makes systemisation and installing a culture of systems-thinking in your business especially challenging is that the beneficial effects aren't always felt instantly. And when the impact is finally felt, the results are so far-reaching that it can be hard to quantify the positive results in one or two key metrics. The impact is felt across the entire company.

Other focus areas of business may provide rapid and obvious measurable benefits. For example, when you create a new ad campaign, you know very quickly whether you're generating leads or burning cash. If it's the former, you know you're doing something right and you double down. If it's the latter, you tweak things and try again. It's a simple equation, the feedback is swift and the results can be easily translated into an appropriate action.

What's challenging is that installing systems doesn't always provide that kind of instant feedback. There's often a noticeable lag to the results, and it may take weeks or even months before you can see their effects.

That's not to mention that the real magic occurs even further down the line when you layer the positive effects of multiple systems, with each system saving you a little time here and a little extra efficiency there. Changing your company culture takes time, but when you add up all the wins, the breakthroughs are unparalleled. Your team and clients are happier, efficiency skyrockets and, most importantly, you win back hours, days, weeks and months of your most valuable asset … time.

As cliché as it is, I'm sure we'd all agree that time is your most valuable asset. Everyone has limited supply and once it's gone, it's gone.

So beware of chasing the bright, shiny objects – while the appeal of the quick win is strong, it's rarely where you will see the biggest returns. You need to slow down in order to speed up. It's this lag time that causes most people to lose their way and why SYSTEMology requires counterintuitive thinking. It's going to require a lot of patience and the discipline to stay the course, but you will be well rewarded for your efforts.

In time, everything will come together. Certain elements of your job will either take a fraction of the time they used to take to complete, or you will delegate your responsibilities entirely. Before you know it, your business will consistently deliver its core products and services, to a very high standard, without your involvement. You will have created a scalable and saleable asset.

The secret is to remove the biggest bottleneck within your business … YOU – the business owner!

How SYSTEMology works

SYSTEMology is a seven-stage process that is designed to identify and create the critical systems within your business. You'll learn to organise them, get your team following them and continue to optimise them. Here are the seven stages we'll work through:

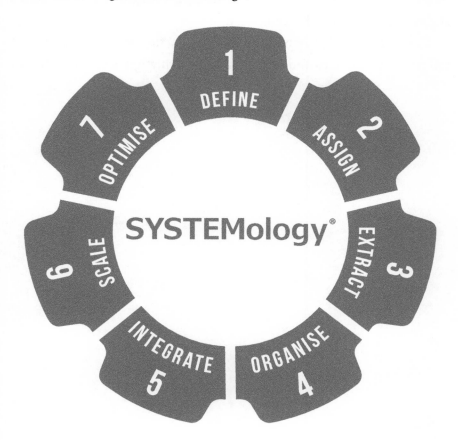

IMPORTANT NOTE: The book itself includes an action plan so that at the end of every chapter you will know exactly what to work on next. That said, if this is your first time reading, it is suggested you read through the entire book first – before taking any action! This ensures you understand the complete methodology.

You will recognise the order of the seven stages is important, and while it has been designed to be implemented chronologically, some knowledge from later chapters will help with the implementation of earlier chapters.

For example, the integration stage is all about getting your team's buy-in to your new, systemised way of doing business – obviously, some of these strategies will be helpful in getting people involved in the earlier stages of extraction and organisation.

So, read through the book first, then on the second time around, follow the action steps and start your implementation. It's time to dive in.

Define

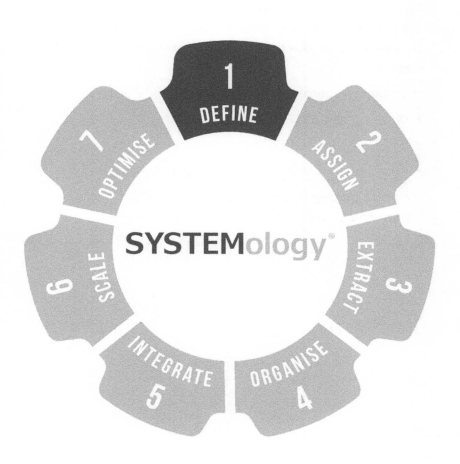

"Define" Chapter Summary

The first stage in SYSTEMology is to reduce the overwhelm. In this chapter, we will take the seemingly epic task of systemising your entire business and identify only the most critical systems. You don't need hundreds of them to systemise your business. You simply need to pick one target audience, one central product or service, and to define the Critical Client Flow (CCF).

The goal of this chapter is to identify 10–15 systems as a starting point for your systemisation journey. Who knows, it may even open your eyes to parts of your process you never even considered.

Highlights from this chapter include:

- *How and why SYSTEMology was born.*

- *What are business systems, and why they matter.*

- *How overcomplicating systems can hold you back.*

- *How to quickly and easily identify the critical few systems that drive your business.*

Define

**You will need to create hundreds of
systems to systemise a business.**

I CAN THINK OF A NUMBER OF MOMENTS in my life that turned out to be far more impactful than I realised at the time. But the one most relevant to the book you're reading was when my wife and I discovered that we were pregnant.

Like most parents-to-be, it had a profound impact on my outlook on … well … everything.

I was going to be a father. I was going to have a son. My son was going to have a father. All of which, now that I write it down, doesn't seem that profound. But at the time it was like discovering the world was secretly run by shape-shifting aliens.

Everything looked and felt different. The lens through which I saw the world was completely new and from that moment all of my experiences, plans, dreams and hopes were from an entirely different perspective.

One of the first things I realised was that my lifestyle had to change. Obviously, it was going to change in many ways, whether I wanted it to or not, but I had some control over how I reacted to those changes. And the biggest part of my life that I needed to adjust was my work life.

At the time, I was running a digital agency called Melbourne SEO Services. We helped businesses with their online presence through things like search engine optimisation (SEO), paid advertising and content marketing. Like most agencies, we worked with lots of different clients in many different industries, so we depended on a high level of campaign customisation.

I'd been working in this business for over ten years and, at that point, I was working at least 60–70 hours a week. I was trapped on the hamster wheel of finding clients, delivering for clients, maintaining relationships and then circling back around to getting new clients again. Each part of my job was critical and required my constant attention.

But now …

How could I possibly spend that number of hours at the office and still have time to be there for my boy? I didn't want to be one of those dads who's always too busy – too busy to walk my son to school, too busy to watch his footy games, too busy to help him with his homework.

Even if I shifted my office and worked primarily from home, the number of hours I would need to put into my business wouldn't change significantly. I'd be physically present but mentally absent. Which, to my mind, amounts to much the same thing.

On top of all that, I was incredibly stressed out a lot of the time. My role in the business was such that it literally couldn't work without me. I had plenty of great employees doing fantastic work, but I was the one who held it all together.

It was like the business was a huge clockwork machine, and I was a cog in the middle that kept all the different elements connected and moving. I enjoyed the work and I was – and still am – proud of what the digital agency produced for its clients. But it placed a lot of pressure on me and, frankly, I didn't want my son to grow up in a house with an absent father.

It wasn't even a question. Somehow, I had to change the way in which I did business.

At the time, our being pregnant didn't present itself as an opportunity to change and improve my business. It was an opportunity to find a new kind of happiness and grow a warm, loving family home, where business was going to take a backseat to those priorities.

But with the wonder that is hindsight, I now realise that without that motivation to significantly change my work situation and to do so quickly, I might still be working crazy hours, moving ever closer to a life of high blood pressure and burnout.

Being pregnant became a defining moment in my life, and as it turned out, for my business.

You've heard it said that necessity is the mother of invention. Well, for me, fatherhood necessitated invention. I literally had to invent a way to build a business that worked without me.

You might think the obvious answer would be to simply sell my business, downsize it or even start from scratch with something simpler and less time intensive. Yet I wasn't ready to let go of what I'd built up over the course of ten years.

And even if I'd wanted to sell the business, I would have had a hard time doing so. No one would be keen to purchase a business that is entirely dependent on the person who's leaving. I would first need to restructure the business so it could function without me at the helm.

Which would solve my problem anyway.

That was the ideal scenario: I keep my business (and the income it provides) but I reorganise and systemise my business so that I don't need to be involved on a day-to-day basis.

Was such a thing even possible? If you're the critical cog in your own business, you know only too well how difficult such an endeavour looks at first, second and even third glance. When you're an entrepreneur who builds a business from the ground up, so much of the operation relies on your specific talents that it initially seems like an impossibility that it could run without you.

That was my point of view as well. What would it take for me to engineer such a paradigm shift, and exactly how long would it take for me to accomplish such a feat?

As it turned out, it took around twelve months.

By that time, I'd systemised almost all the key elements of my business AND hired a CEO to replace me at the top of the business. I'm still involved in the sense that I meet regularly with my replacement to discuss issues and make suggestions on critical issues, and while I prefer my CEO to make almost all the key decisions, when it's absolutely necessary I reserve the right to have the final say.

My involvement with the business is about as minimal as it's possible to be, and it all happened before my son was more than a few months old.

Critically, the whole operation has proved to be sustainable. I work from home, primarily on my new business venture (of which SYSTEMology is just one element), and if one of my kids – yes, I have two of 'em now – wants to knock on my office door and tell me about their day or ask me to go outside to play catch, that's absolutely fine. They often make cameo appearances in my Zoom meetings and can be heard in the background of my podcast episodes. This is the life I have shaped for myself.

Like I said, the right motivation is a powerful factor. Achieving the same results in your business might take longer or, if you have the right incentives (and a solid plan), you might be able to accomplish this faster.

But for now, just know that no matter how entrenched in your business you may feel yourself to be, SYSTEMology will help you find the freedom you're looking for. Or maybe the freedom you need.

So, that's your first step in applying SYSTEMology to your business …

Get pregnant!

Actually, no, don't do that. I mean, do it if you want to; being a parent is endlessly rewarding. But don't get pregnant just to create motivation.

For most people, I would imagine that the prospect of a better-functioning business, a reduction in work and stress and the potential to extract yourself from operations (or even sell the business) is motivation enough.

Your real first step is to begin to get clear on what's holding you in the business.

In Michael E. Gerber's original book, *The E-Myth*, he explains the 'entrepreneurial myth': the false belief most small business owners hold that just because they understand the technical work of a business, they can successfully run a business that does that technical work.

The truth is there's more to running a business than just doing the technical work. There are sales, marketing, financials, human resources and management, just to name a few. That's what makes business so challenging. Moreover, at every turn, the business owner is solving problems and, as a result, they get really great at problem-solving.

The trap is that this skill of solving problems then leads to the business owner unconsciously training their team to become dependent on them. Instead of empowering their team to solve problems, they're the knight in shining armour who always saves the day. This, in turn, makes them even better at problem-solving and causes team members to become even more dependent.

It's a horrible cycle that's almost impossible to break.

So, how the heck do you remove a business owner from a business so dependent on them? What's the secret?

The secret is systems.

What is a system?

A system – also known as a process, a procedure, standard operating procedures (SOPs), work instructions, a 'how-to' document or workflow – is just **a series of linear steps that, when followed, produces a predictable outcome.** This definition works on the smallest level where a system may be a detailed step-by-step instruction, all the way up to a high-level system that shows how an overall project fits together. A system may be unconscious and undocumented, but it still has a series of moves that produces a result.

Whether we're aware of it or not, we all have systems that we create and use in different areas of our life. We might not be aware of the existence of those systems, but that doesn't make us immune to their results. For example, if we have poor health systems (we eat junk food and don't exercise), over a period of time we will become overweight – whether we knew this would be the outcome or not.

In short, not knowing will not save you.

In business it's the same. Poor recruiting systems will lead to staffing issues, poor financial systems will lead to cash flow issues and poor marketing systems will lead to lead flow issues. All problems within business are, ultimately, caused by poorly performing systems.

And the first step to improving them is to become aware of their existence. See your business as a collection of interconnected systems.

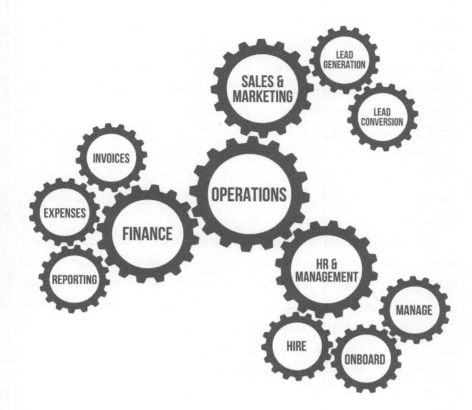

Keep your systems simple

SYSTEMology is built on the foundation of keeping things simple. We start by breaking your business down into its component parts, identifying the critical points and then building those core components into simple systems.

The key to making this work is simplicity. You're not a Fortune 500 company, you don't have hundreds of staff and you don't win any awards for making your business more complex.

To remind you to keep it simple, I will sometimes use the word 'overview' to stop you from going too granular. For example, as part of SYSTEMology, you will create an 'overview system' to outline the high-level steps in the delivery of your product or service. This will typically include many smaller steps and components. It may be supported by a range of more detailed documented systems, it may include more than one person and it may have a time delay between the steps. But remember to view it as an overview – so just capture the top level and keep it simple.

If you're a detail-oriented person, or worse, a perfectionist, YOUR challenge at this stage is to hold yourself in check and avoid getting too granular.

My epiphany on this subject came from a good friend of mine by the name of Mike Rhodes – he's a former E-Myth coach, owns a company called WebSavvy and is a super sharp guy.

He's a lover of systems and really learnt the value of a systemised business when he sold his first business, an internet café in New Zealand. Mike created a manual that described every detail of how to manage the business and keep it running smoothly so that, when he eventually found a buyer, he was able to get top dollar. It was an easier and more profitable sell BECAUSE the new owner knew the business would still be able to operate when Mike was no longer running it.

After selling up, he moved to Australia and started a new life and business.

Through Mike's work as an E-Myth coach, he fell in love with the power of Google advertising and set up a business to help other companies leverage this opportunity. He continued to create systems and processes for this new business except, this time, he decided to go all-out. He documented every aspect of his business and literally created hundreds of systems ... he even created an index of all these systems that he stuck to the wall of his office.

We shared office space for a while, and I used to look through the window and see this great big wall of systems. There were pages and pages, each line representing a system with its own unique steps and processes. He wanted everyone to see it as a reminder that they were only a few steps away from finding the relevant system for their job at hand.

Sounds like a great idea, right? But in reality, it bombed.

It was too overwhelming. Employees couldn't make sense of it. And, in addition, because the business centred around digital marketing, his systems were prone to change almost on a daily basis. As you could imagine, keeping it up to date was an almost impossible task.

This taught me – and Mike – a valuable lesson about systemising a business ...

Don't over-document your business

Just as in many other areas of life, the Pareto principle (sometimes called the 80/20 rule) applies here. This is a well-established theory by Italian economist Vilfredo Pareto, who found that 80 per cent of the effects of a thing come from 20 per cent of the causes. For instance, many businesses, when they look closely, discover things like...

- 80 per cent of their leads come from 20 per cent of their advertisements.

- 80 per cent of their sales come from 20 per cent of their salespeople.
- 80 per cent of client complaints come from 20 per cent of their client base.
- 80 per cent of all sick days are taken by 20 per cent of their employees.

Once you're aware of this principle, you'll start to see it at work everywhere, and business systems are no exception.

Just 20 per cent of the systems you create will provide 80 per cent of your efficiency wins.

How do you identify the critical few systems?

Bearing in mind that one of the primary objectives of SYSTEMology is to have your business deliver its central product independent of the business owner, do you think you could explain HOW the core of your business works on the back of a napkin?

Do you know the minimum viable systems required to consistently bring in new business, convert those leads to clients and then deliver your product/service?

If not, don't worry ...

In SYSTEMology this is step one and we have a process (surprise, surprise) to uncover these core systems. It's called the Critical Client Flow™ (CCF). It takes about twenty minutes to complete, identifies the critical few and provides tremendous insights. Through the process you will see the 'holes' within your business and it will help you develop laser-like focus on what needs to be systemised.

To be clear, you will not create anything new at this stage; you're merely uncovering what you're already doing in a format that is frequently eye-opening. To understand the concept, all you need to recognise is that there is a path your client and business follows to deliver your core product/service. We'll use a simple template to help you identify this flow.

Head to www.SYSTEMology.com/resources and download the CCF template. Print it out, start at the top and let's work through it together, filling in the blanks.

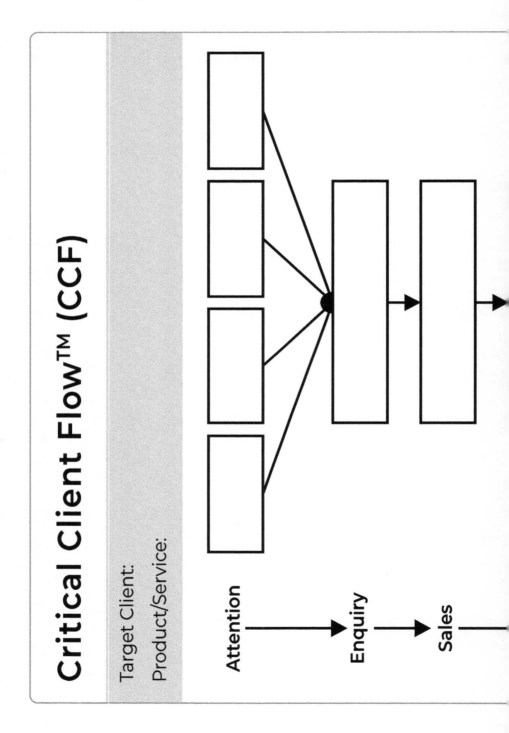

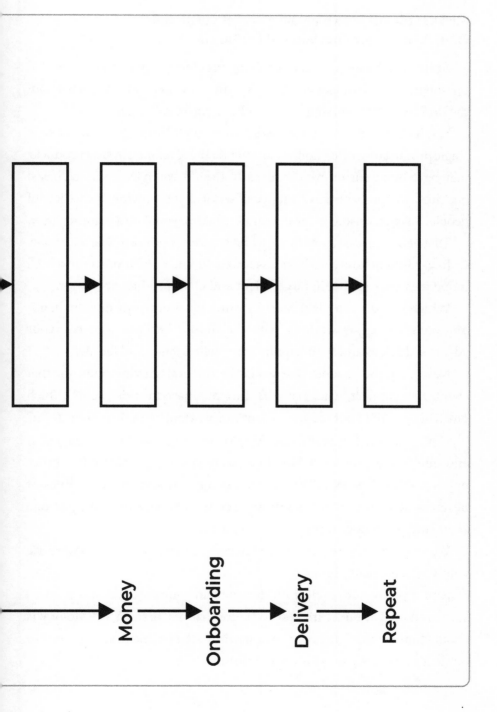

Step #1: Identify ONE primary target client and ONE primary product you sell to that client.

At its core, business is about solving problems – and you're rewarded for solving those problems – therefore the first step is to be clear about the problem you're solving and for whom you're solving it.

Yes, it's true, very few businesses have a single target client, let alone a single product or service. Some, particularly those selling physical products, may have hundreds or even thousands. Even if you have a service-based business, you probably have a range of services you provide to a variety of people. So, systemising every potential scenario would be a daunting task.

That being the case, for our very first step, we're going to select just one.

Regardless of how your business is structured, or the industry in which it operates, pick just ONE target client and ONE product or service.

Which one do you pick? Start by thinking about your dream clients. The ones you enjoy working with the most. The ones who pay your advertised prices and then happily refer their friends and family.

Next, pick the product that would be the best starting point for that client. Ask yourself, what is a great first purchase for this client? Which one will open the door for you to continue working with them long-term?

Now I know, for many, the idea of picking just one target client and one primary product feels like you're closing yourself off to other opportunities. However, I'm not suggesting you stop all other lines of business. Remember, this is just an exercise, and starting with just one client and product ensures you stay focused.

We can't systemise everything on day one, but we can start to systemise your Critical Client Flow.

And if you're not yet clear on the problem your products and services solve and for whom … it's best to figure that out first. SYSTEMology is about cloning what's already working within the business, so you need to be clear on where your sweet spot is located.

Here are some examples of what you're looking for:

- If you're a bookkeeper, your target clients might be farmers and your primary service is an initial financial audit.

- If you're a digital agency, maybe you serve franchisors and your primary service is building them a new website.

- If you're a rock 'n' roll music clothing store, you may target teenagers who like rock music and your primary product is a heavy metal T-shirt.

Just focus on ONE central client and ONE primary product or service. Once you're clear, fill in the blanks at the top of the worksheet.

Step #2: Define your Critical Client Flow.

There are key stages your clients and business go through to deliver your core product – from how you first get the attention of your target clients, through to delivering your product to them and hopefully turning them into repeat clients. The CCF identifies this as a series of linear events.

Note: The difference between a CCF and a typical 'client journey' is that it also focuses on the requirements of the business to deliver your product. If you already have your client journey mapped out, that's great; no doubt it will help you complete the CCF. But they're not the same.

Of course, every business is going to have a slightly different series of steps, but broadly speaking they'll include most or all of the components below. Your job is to fill in the blanks.

Before you begin, there are three rules to keep in mind:

1. Don't overthink this.

2. Don't go into detail – two or three words to label a step is all you need.

3. Only populate the CCF with activities you are currently doing.

Let's look at each component, starting from the top.

Attention: How do people learn about your business?

Search engine traffic? Pay-per-click ads? Podcast advertising? Direct mail? Speaking engagements? Referrals?

There are literally hundreds of ways to generate new business, but as you go through the CCF, the question is: *How are you currently doing it?* Avoid filling in the blanks with things you'd *like* to be doing. Just list your primary methods of getting your prospects' attention.

Enquiry: When someone is ready to enquire about your products, how do they do it?

Is it through an inbound call, do they submit a web enquiry, or both?

Sales: Your prospect has shown interest in your wares and now they're primed to become a client. What happens next?

Do they bring an item to the checkout counter? Do they add items to their online shopping cart and click on the 'checkout' button? Do they call you up to make an appointment? Do you issue proposals? How do you close the sale?

Just name the typical process, keeping in mind this exercise is for ONE core product being purchased by ONE specific target client. Don't try to describe every possible sales process.

Money: How do you collect payment?

This could be an easy step – cash or card. Or, if you're a service provider, you might invoice before the work is carried out. Or afterwards. Or a combination of the two.

Onboarding: How do you get your clients started?

This could be as simple as putting the goods in a bag, or it could be an in-depth onboarding process involving questionnaires, setting up projects in a project management software and assigning the account manager.

With service-based businesses, you may find it helpful to identify how new client projects are set up as opposed to how you deliver the actual work. This ensures nothing is missed, expectations are set and there's a smooth transition from the sales team to the operations team.

You could probably list a whole bunch of systems here, but keep it simple. Don't list more than one or two steps. We'll build up the details later in the process.

Delivery: How is the work completed?

A physical business might just involve handing the product over. But an ecommerce operation could cover ordering stock, checking it off, packaging it up and shipping it out.

For a service-based operation – a bookkeeper, for instance – this would include how to extract the initial data from the client's accounting software, how it's interpreted and how it's delivered to the client.

Oftentimes, this step in particular gets people's minds racing as they think about the multitude of steps in this process. Rest assured that we're going to capture all the details later – for now, we keep it simple.

Repeat or referral: Last, but not least, how do you go about encouraging clients to either remain a client or come back again to make additional purchases?

If you're in the business of selling coffins or some other product where you're usually making a one-time sale, think in terms of referrals. How do you encourage your clients to send you new business?

I always find it easier to write out this whole process by hand, using the worksheet. The goal here is to break your business down into a linear series of steps that your clients move through when working with your business. It should consist of no more than 7–12 steps.

There's a good chance you'll experience some 'a-ha' moments as you go through this exercise, because it often highlights areas of weakness and helps to explain why certain issues appear within your business. By capturing only what you are actually doing, any holes become immediately apparent.

If you have trouble creating consistent leads, for example, it's probable you don't have multiple methods for gaining your clients' attention. If you're having cash flow issues, you may have poor invoicing systems. If you have trouble with clients who constantly follow up and micromanage you and your team, you probably have a poor onboarding sequence that fails to set expectations.

These insights will guide you in later chapters on where to focus, but for now we're just concentrating on how your business currently operates.

It's not a problem if you have to massage the CCF a little to suit your situation. I know everyone's business is a little different and there's never a 'one size fits all'. As long as tweaking the template doesn't involve blowing it up to more than a dozen steps, you'll be just fine.

If you have ended up with more than twelve steps, have another go at creating something shorter and more concise. You could, for instance, combine some of the steps together, especially if they're all being carried out by the same person or department.

As an example, if you own a retail store where there isn't really a separate 'onboarding' stage for new clients, this could be combined with the delivery step.

The goal, ultimately, is to explain in simple terms how your business works from start to finish, in a linear fashion.

Step #3: Share your completed CCF.

You can then test your result by sharing your creation with someone outside of the business – preferably someone who knows roughly what your business does but isn't directly involved. If you can show them your CCF and they can understand it WITHOUT you having to talk them through the steps in great detail, you're in good shape. If they find your creation confusing or too complex, have another go and simplify further.

Here are a few sample CCFs to give you some ideas.

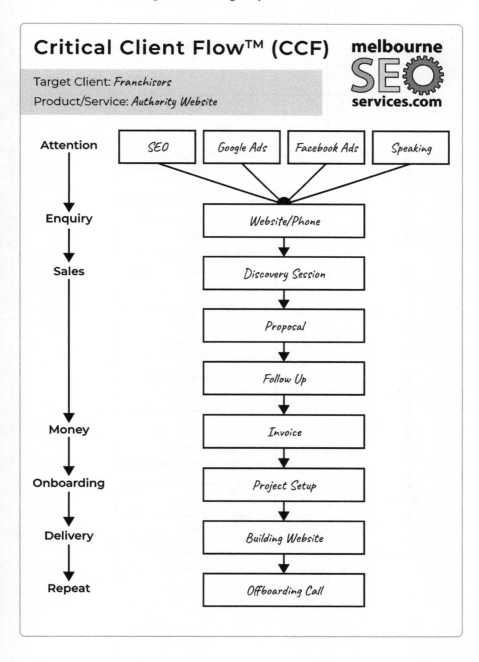

Critical Client Flow™ (CCF)

melbourne SEO services.com

Target Client: *Franchisors*
Product/Service: *Authority Website*

Attention	SEO · Google Ads · Facebook Ads · Speaking
Enquiry	Website/Phone
Sales	Discovery Session
	Proposal
	Follow Up
Money	Invoice
Onboarding	Project Setup
Delivery	Building Website
Repeat	Offboarding Call

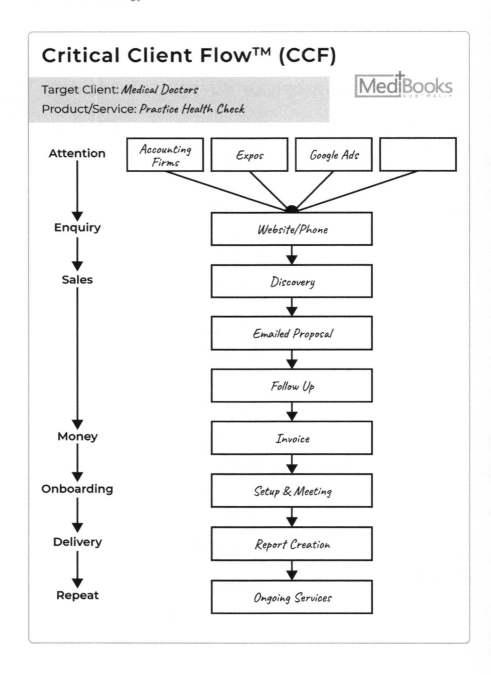

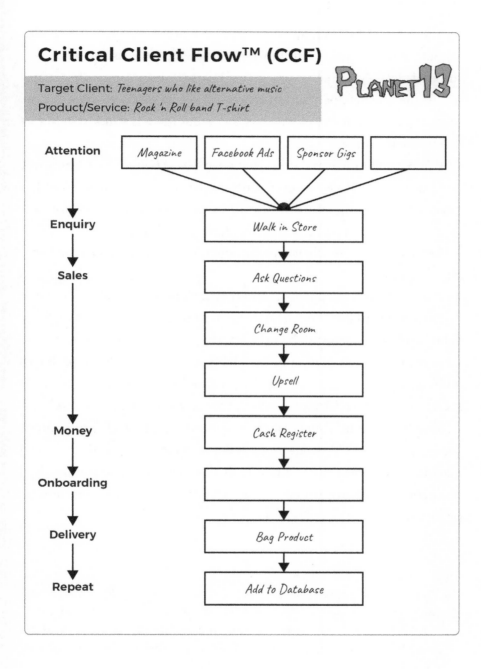

Critical Client Flow™ (CCF)

Target Client: *Teenagers who like alternative music*
Product/Service: *Rock 'n Roll band T-shirt*

PLANET13

Attention — Magazine | Facebook Ads | Sponsor Gigs | [blank]

Enquiry — Walk in Store

Sales — Ask Questions

Change Room

Upsell

Money — Cash Register

Onboarding — [blank]

Delivery — Bag Product

Repeat — Add to Database

The last example might sound odd but it's actually the CCF that I would have created if I still owned Planet 13, the rock 'n' roll music-inspired clothing store that was one of my first business ventures. It may not fit the template perfectly, it may not have an in-depth sales system, invoicing system or even delivery system, but there is still a system that can be documented.

Before you jump in and think, *But my business is different*, let me agree and say yes, it is. However, every business has a Critical Client Flow. I've never once, over the years of helping hundreds of people perform this exercise, found a business where I couldn't identify their CCF.

Remember … one client, one product, one journey. Document that and you have a CCF.

It doesn't need to be perfect and it doesn't need to be all-inclusive. It just needs to exist and provide some focus into how your business delivers value to your clients. And the really exciting thing is, once you systemise this, you're well on your way to solving your target clients' problems without key person dependency. This is also the first step to dramatically increasing your capacity and ability to create a scalable money machine.

Yes, there will be a range of other systems we'll look at further down the line, but the CCF strikes right at the heart of the myth that you will need to create hundreds and hundreds of systems to build a systemised business. This is a false belief, and the fact is you will get tremendous wins by focusing on just the critical few.

Would it be helpful to watch a live creation of the CCF? Watch Nick Griffiths from MediBooks (an Australia-based bookkeeping firm) as he walks you through the creation of his. Sometimes all it takes is seeing someone else follow the process for you to 'get it'.

www.SYSTEMology.com/resources

Case Study   Ecosystem Solutions

Gary McMahon founded Ecosystem Solutions in 2005. The small business helps a range of clients, from governments and corporations to families, in the highly specialised niche of ecological consulting. Demand grew very quickly.

The company's success came at a steep cost to Gary, though. Years of working 100–110 hours per week jeopardised his health, his relationship with his family and the quality of his work.

He hired staff and tried to expand to lighten the load, but he was still going at the same rate. He was the quintessential bottleneck in his business. Every tool and all the training he could find didn't help, either. Nothing solved his problem. He knew he needed to do something, even had an inkling that it had something to do with systems, but he didn't know what.

"This is my only hope," he said when he came across SYSTEMology. He fell in love with the promise of complete business reliability. Surely this was his golden ticket.

He began implementing the steps one by one. The CCF, especially, was a "game changer," allowing him and his team to visualise the bottlenecks. He eventually used his CCF to onboard new team members and create a cohesive brand identity.

Through implementing the SYSTEMology approach, "profitability increased approximately 80 per cent." But his greatest win? A three-week holiday with his family -- for the first time in his entire working life.

When asked what it means to have a systemised business, Gary said, "Peace of mind."

"It's like I've lost fifty kilos! And I've got a life. It's bizarre."

Today, Gary can leave for a training or family day any day of the week and trust that his team can handle everything while he's away – probably even better than if he did the work himself.

"Define" action steps

- **Download the Critical Client Flow template from www.SYSTEMology.com/resources.**

  ▶ Step #1: Identify ONE primary target client and ONE primary product you sell to that client.

  ▶ Step #2: Define your Critical Client Flow.

  ▶ Step #3: Share your completed CCF.

Assign

"Assign" Chapter Summary

The second stage in SYSTEMology is to recognise that the knowledge of how to do a task to a great standard already exists within your team. In this chapter, you will locate the knowledge and, where possible, take the business owner out of the equation. The fact is, if you're serious about removing key person dependency, it's time to assign the responsibility of systems development to capable team members.

Highlights from this chapter include:

- *Why the business owner is typically the worst person to develop systems and processes.*

- *How to quickly and easily create a systems development action plan detailing who is doing what by when.*

- *Why modelling your best team members is the best-kept secret to rapid systems development.*

Assign

The business owner is the only one who can create the systems.

MANY BUSINESS OWNERS BELIEVE THAT for something to be done 'right' they must do it themselves. The truth is, if you're the only person who can do a task, there's something wrong with the way your business is built, and you have fallen into a trap. You must keep pushing yourself to evolve through this trap. I still occasionally fall into it myself.

I freely admit that I'm a recovering micromanager. In my old business (the digital agency), I learned to put good people in charge and let go… but with my newest business, it's become easy to slip into old habits (especially when it's something I'm passionate about).

Case in point: I was preparing a workshop for some of my clients, and I decided to check over the room that we'd booked. I just wanted to get a feel for the room and visualise how everything would come together. Now, when I arrived, I started to panic that the space we'd been assigned was too small for the number of people we were expecting.

Bear in mind that it was a Friday and the event was taking place the following Wednesday. The venue had told me that all other rooms were booked and I'd have to wait until Monday to chat with our events contact.

Guess what I did? I went into full-on stress mode.

I was calling different team members, sending emails, sending text messages ...

"Things aren't right!"

"It's going to be too crowded."

"We're not going to be able to seat everyone."

When I got home, my wife tried to reassure me that we would find a way to make it work, but I'd already sent out all the messages and worked myself up.

Monday morning rolled around, and I got an email from the team member managing the event on my behalf. Even before I'd sent my panicky emails, they'd already spotted the large attendee numbers and had arranged for us to be moved into a bigger room.

All the while I was getting myself worked up, sending emails and messages to my team and interrupting their Friday evening, everything was already taken care of.

This isn't me saying that the answer is to stop caring and paying attention to the details. This is me sharing how often business owners can get in the way of good team members and processes, and unnecessarily complicate things.

Once you get to the point where you're no longer the heart of the business, interfering with the daily operations is rarely a good idea.

With the benefit of hindsight, what I should have done was send one text to the person on our team in charge of the event and let them handle it. In this case, they would have let me know they had already taken care of it. Case closed.

How about you? Do you believe that for things to be done right you need to be involved? It's okay to admit it – that's the first step to recovery. Take it from one who's already wrestled with this over the years.

You might not be the best person for this job

When systemising businesses, it's a common misconception that it's the business owner who will need to be the one creating the systems because they know how they want things done. One of the many problems with this way of thinking is that we all know systems are important ... but they're never urgent. So, like all 'non-urgent' tasks, no one ever gets to them.

The truth is the business owner is typically the worst person to be documenting systems.

Phew! Breathe a sigh of relief! This is good news for just about every small business owner on the planet. Let's break this habit, right now, of thinking we need to be the one doing everything ourselves.

There are plenty of knowledgeable people you work with who might (at the very least) be able to start the process. So, let me ask you, what would you do if you had to systemise your business without heavy involvement from the business owner?

It's time to identify the key departments, the key team members within those departments and where the knowledge already resides within your business. Once we know who has the knowledge (avoiding the business owner where possible), it's simply a matter of capturing what they're already doing.

Your business is already functioning, so we're not looking to reinvent the wheel or craft a perfect process right from day one. We simply want to capture what is already being done well. Huge wins can be gained by creating consistency within your team.

To do this we need to create your Departments, Responsibilities & Team Chart™ (DRTC). It's a little bit like creating an organisation chart, except not really. If you already have an organisation chart, you can use it to help, but we're creating something simpler. The purposes of the CCF and the DRTC are to give you some focus and pin down who we need to work with to extract the knowledge we need.

The DRTC sits nicely alongside your CCF. And, as with the previous step, try not to overthink the task or get too bogged down in the details.

I know I've said it before, but I can't say it enough: complexity is the enemy of systemisation. You may even hear a little voice in your head trying to convince you that what you've created is too simple to work effectively.

Ignore that voice.

Stick to the path and you'll get the results you're looking for.

Head to www.SYSTEMology.com/resources and download the Departments, Responsibilities & Team Chart (DRTC) template.

Departments, Responsibilities & Team Chart™ (DRTC)

Departments											
Responsibilities											
Team											

Step #1: Identify key departments.

We begin by dividing your business into departments and listing them along the top of the worksheet. Think about how your business might be described based on the different functions that make it work.

For example:

- Marketing – covers all the systems related to how new leads and prospects are generated for the business. This is how you gain the attention of your target audience.
- Sales – covers all the systems related to how prospects are then converted into clients.
- Operations – covers everything to do with how your product is created and delivered for your client.
- Finance – covers all aspects of money moving in and out of the business.
- Human resources (HR) – covers everything to do with attracting, hiring, onboarding and managing the team.
- Management – covers the systems for strategic direction, goal setting and the leadership team.

Don't get hung up on details such as whether some departments should be listed individually or combined. For example, maybe you'd like to put 'sales and marketing' together or maybe you would like to create an additional department for 'administration' or 'stock ordering'. It really doesn't matter, since we're not setting anything in stone.

Similarly, with your naming, go with what makes sense to your business. Some people call their operations 'client fulfilment' while others call it 'delivery'. Go with your gut instinct and, once you have a list, write them out in a row at the top of the worksheet. If you're not sure, just use those I've listed.

Cross-check your CCF to make sure all the steps you identified there have a department that they would clearly fit under.

STAGE TWO: ASSIGN   65

Below is a typical set of departments.

Departments						
	Marketing	Sales	Finance	Operations	HR	Management

Step #2: Assign the responsibilities of each department.

At this step we're pretty much just breaking down every stage of the CCF and assigning it to a department. There's no rocket science here.

Again, adhere closely to your CCF and list those steps in the relevant columns. For example, on your CCF, you may have identified a few methods to capture your audience's attention (SEO, Google Ads, Facebook Ads, speaking) – list all of those under the marketing column.

Here's an example from my digital agency.

Departments						
	Marketing	Sales	Finance	Operations	HR	Management
Responsibilities						
	SEO	Web / Phone	Invoice	Project setup		
	Google Ads	Discovery Session		Building website		
	Facebook Ads	Proposal				
	Speaking	Follow up				
		Offboarding call				

Step #3: Assign department heads.

At this step, we're looking for people within your team to take ownership of each department. As we said earlier, this isn't an organisation chart and its primary purpose is to help with the systemisation of your business. That said, if you already have an organisation chart, great! Just use your previously assigned department heads. If you don't have one, that's fine too.

A department head is simply the person who will take ultimate responsibility when decisions around that department need to be made. List the name in the row marked 'team'. It's perfectly fine if some people are the heads of more than one department. For very small businesses, this is a given.

That said, if you find the business owner's name is listed at the top of most or all of the departments, this could mean one of two things: either you're desperately in need of SYSTEMology, or you're not quite ready to systemise.

For SYSTEMology to have a marked impact on your business, you need to have at least a few team members or contractors with whom you work on a regular basis. This ensures this whole process doesn't fall on the shoulders of the business owner and you will get some leverage from the systems you create.

If you're still a one-man band, it's best to focus on perfecting your messaging, getting clients and building a reputation for delivering great results for your clients. This will allow you to build a small team before you build your systems. SYSTEMology will replicate what's already working but you must get some traction first.

Now, if you already have a team and you still find the business owner at the head of almost all of the departments, that's okay too. We'll work on this. For now, just be aware that the goal we're working towards is removing them from those key positions. As before, capture things as they are, not how you'd like them to be.

Departments						
	Marketing	Sales	Finance	Operations	HR	Management
Responsibilities						
	SEO	Web / Phone	Invoice	Project setup		
	Google Ads	Discovery Session		Building website		
	Facebook Ads	Proposal				
	Speaking	Follow up				
		Offboarding call				
Team						
	Jillian	Melissa	Sally	Grace	Melissa	Melissa

Step #4: Identify additional knowledgeable workers.

Next up, for each department brainstorm any other, what we'll call, 'knowledgeable workers'. Clearly, your department heads are knowledgeable, but chances are they're also busy ... so it's good to know who else holds the knowledge within your organisation.

For example, under your marketing department you might have identified one of the critical responsibilities as handling incoming enquiries. If you have an admin person who answers the phone and directs your inbound email enquiries to the relevant person, they would be identified as a knowledgeable worker and should be listed accordingly.

Note: You don't need to list every team member; just those with critical knowledge or expertise that is directly involved in the systems you identified in your CCF.

Once you've finished this task, you'll have a list of team members who are going to be vital when it comes to extracting and developing your systems. Who knows, some of these team members could also be candidates for eventually leading a department.

Continuing our example, here's how it's all coming together.

Departments, Responsibilities & Team Chart™ (DRTC)						
Departments						
	Marketing	Sales	Finance	Operations	HR	Management
Responsibilities						
	SEO	Web / Phone	Invoice	Project setup		
	Google Ads	Discovery Session		Building website		
	Facebook Ads	Proposal				
	Speaking	Follow up				
		Offboarding call				
Team						
	Jillian	Melissa	Sally	Grace	Melissa	Melissa
	Dave	Jillian	Melissa	Web: Nikki	Dave	Dave
	SEO: Grace			Video: Max		
	SEM: Paul			SEM: Paul		

Step #5: Assign critical systems to knowledgeable workers.

Great, you're almost there! You now know where most of the critical knowledge is stored inside your business. In this step, we're going to turn this into an action plan, listing the key systems and the individuals that are best placed to help develop those systems.

This step is best explained by looking at the worksheet. Let me share my pre-populated example.

Systems Assign Sheet

Department	System Name	Description	Knowledgeable Worker
Marketing	SEO	How to write and optimise a blog post	Grace
Marketing	Google Ads	How to review our account monthly	Paul
Marketing	Facebook Ads	How to run a Facebook advertisement to webinar	Trevor
Marketing	Speaking	How to identify and outreach to potential events	Dave
Sales	Web / Phone	Handle inbound enquiry via website or phone	Jillian
Sales	Discovery Session	Script for discovery sessions	Melissa
Sales	Proposal	How to prepare a proposal, send to client, email template	Jillian
Sales	Follow up	How to follow up leads, how often, email templates	Jillian
Finance	Invoice	How to issue an invoice via Xero	Sally
Operations	Project setup	How to setup project or job for smooth management	Melissa
Operations	Building website	Overview system detailing the main step in delivery	Melissa
Sales	Offboarding call	Sales process to make additional sales	Melissa

Transfer all of the key data you've already populated into part two of the worksheet. Copy across the departments, system titles and a sentence or two that gives some detail about what you imagine the system will cover.

Avoid the temptation to write loads of details here (this comes later). You're just looking for a brief description (not more than a few sentences) of what the system is intended to achieve.

This might be one of the hardest parts of this step because deciding what is and isn't critical can be difficult. If, for instance, one of your key tasks for getting attention is looking after your social media accounts, there might be a dozen different jobs connected to this and all may seem essential.

It will be tempting to throw your hands up and just list them all, but this won't help your cause. It's possible that, eventually, you will systemise all aspects of this task, but right now you've got to decide what is the 20 per cent that makes all the difference.

Remember, not systemising a job doesn't mean it's suddenly going to stop happening. All those social media tasks will keep being completed, just as they are now. This process simply identifies one or two critical systems that are central to those particular responsibilities.

For instance, continuing with the social media example, perhaps identifying, creating and scheduling regular posts to keep your pages active is at the core and will make a perfect system to capture.

Just keep the 80/20 rule top of mind and we'll work on those systems first.

Note: In cases where you're working with a specialist or consultant outside of your business, and they manage that particular task (such as SEO or SEM or bookkeeping), you can work with them to create an overview system that outlines what's being done. Or perhaps they might even have some suggestions for you on what you can do to make their job easier and improve their results.

The final step in this whole process is assigning the knowledgeable worker to each of these systems. This may be the department head or another team member. It very much depends on who has the key skills required to complete that task to a great standard.

This is ultimately the person we'll extract the process from, so ask yourself who does this task and does it to a great standard? In situations where more than one person can do the task, like a sales role, look towards the team member who delivers above average results for that task.

Suggestion: Where possible, avoid adding the business owner's name. Yes, I know business owners can do everything and they can typically do it better than anyone else (or so they believe), but let's take them out of the picture. There will be times this is unavoidable, but do your best. We can always loop them back in further down the line.

Model the best

Part of the genius of this process is that we're going to model your new systems on the best practices of your top performers. This process is then shared with all team members – in so doing, you'll dramatically improve performance across the board.

Perhaps some of the biggest and quickest gains to be made within any business come from uncovering who in the team does a particular task and gets above average results. Then it's simply a matter of extracting what they're doing and teaching others to do the same. This then becomes the new standard and sets the expectation for how best to complete this task.

I've seen this work countless times to great effect, particularly in sales systems. Oftentimes, your top performers are top performers for a reason. They're presenting all the key information and answering objections in a certain way. They're following up and giving prospects everything they need to make a buying decision. They have a system, whether they recognise it or not.

Now imagine how powerful it will be to capture this method and train all the rest of your team to reach this new level. It's easier than you think, and the breakthrough you have been looking for may be right under your nose.

Limit your scope to sharpen your focus

If it feels like I'm trying to constrict your early efforts, then I've succeeded.

What I want is for you to have a clear action plan that is limited in scope and, therefore, will allow you to focus and actually start getting things done. Planning is good, but too much preparation will prevent you from ever acting – you'll be too bogged down in the details and the overwhelm will soon follow.

The systems you've identified are central to how the business makes money, and while you may not have realised it … we've totally annihilated the myth we started with at the beginning of this chapter.

The myth that the business owner will need to be the one who creates all the systems.

The truth is, usually the knowledge already exists in the heads of your team members … we just need a way to extract it.

I know that some people will read this and still won't be able to see this process working without themselves at every level. But sooner or later you will let go. You will trust your team, you will let them step up and you'll be one step closer to the freedom you've been searching for.

Let SYSTEMology guide you through.

Case Study   Absolute Immigration

In operation for almost two decades, Absolute Immigration assists people with immigration and visa processing. In providing a service that is so personally important to their clients, a high degree of accuracy and consistency is critical.

After filling in for a few key team members as they took leave, company director Jamie Lingham discovered that his business had the appearance of five different organisations operating under one roof. Everyone was doing things their own way.

While he knew systemisation was key, he had tried in the past and failed. Then he found SYSTEMology. Almost instantly, he had an 'a-ha' moment that changed the course of his business. Jamie realised he wasn't the best person to drive this initiative.

So he went on a holiday and empowered his team to map the CCF and identify the knowledgeable workers. His operations manager drove the process, and his team then recorded and documented those systems.

The smooth-running machine that Jamie has been shooting for is now a reality and every department is working in a consistent fashion. The robust systems keep every job on track and the firm is now in a position to comfortably increase their workload.

Jamie observed that, "The systems and processes we have ... [enable] our business to move on to the next level ... to scale dramatically, and to handle huge volumes of work, but also ensure that everybody's on the same page."

"Assign" action steps

- **Download and complete the Department, Responsibilities & Team Chart (DRTC) template from www.SYSTEMology.com/resources.**

  ► Step #1: Identify key departments.

  ► Step #2: Assign the responsibilities of each department.

  ► Step #3: Assign department heads.

  ► Step #4: Identify additional knowledgeable workers.

  ► Step #5: Assign critical systems to knowledgeable workers.

STAGE
THREE

Extract

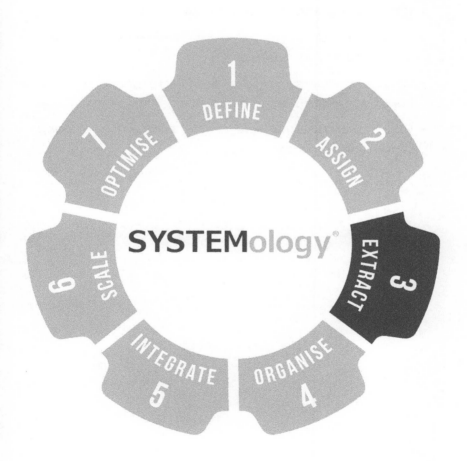

"Extract" Chapter Summary

The third stage in SYSTEMology is to capture the knowledge from your team and turn it into a shareable system. In this chapter, I will quite literally share the system for creating systems. The name sounds funny, but one of the primary reasons people struggle to systemise their business is precisely because they don't have a system to guide them.

Highlights from this chapter include:

- *Why creating systems should ALWAYS be a two-person job.*

- *Rock solid strategies to get 'buy-in' and cooperation from EVERYONE in your business.*

- *What is a systems champion and why they're essential for building a systems-centred business.*

- *Why flowcharts and screenshots suck when creating systems and processes.*

Extract

M Y T H

Creating systems is time-consuming.

Y OU'VE IDENTIFIED THE CRITICAL SYSTEMS in your business, you've assigned key departments and responsibilities, and you've identified where the knowledge resides. Now you need to work with those team members to create long, boring standard operating procedures (SOPs) no one will ever read.

You know the documents I'm talking about. Epic, long, numbered lists, with roman numeral sub-lists, hundreds of bullet points, millions of screenshots and flowcharts no one can edit.

Ahhh … this sounds painful. How the heck are you going to find the time to do this?

Well, if you followed the instructions carefully from the previous chapters and many of these tasks have been assigned to other team members, you could just rule with an iron fist. Yeah, that sounds good. Force your team members to find the time to document their jobs. If they don't like it, you can always fire 'em.

Actually, no, don't do that. That would be idiotic.

You know as well as I do that your best team members are every bit as busy as you and there's a good chance many of them won't relish the idea of creating systems! Do you really want to force them to do something they don't want to do?

Of course not. And you don't have to. Because the SYSTEMology version of creating systems is nothing like anything you've tried before. This is the stage that's going to knock out the biggest myth of all.

That the actual process of creating the systems is time-consuming and painful.

I used to believe this myself until I found a better way.

Before SYSTEMology, back when I was looking to step away from my digital agency, I explained to a mentor of mine how much of a challenge it was to document my systems. Almost without a second thought he suggested, "Why don't you just hire a consultant to create them for you?"

My immediate response, at least in my head, was, "Yeah but I don't want to pay some overpriced consultant to come in and create some documents for parts of my business they know little to nothing about."

But while my initial reaction was to write off the idea, I am a sucker for business shortcuts. I'm always on the lookout for ways to get the best result in the least possible moves. So, the idea that I didn't have to be the one creating the systems was definitely one that I kept coming back to.

Fast forward a few years. After doing things the hard way for way too long, I came up with a spin on the idea. I decided to produce a podcast on which I would interview experts who knew how to solve the problems I was having in my business. Although, I didn't plan on marketing it this way to my guests. Ahem.

If I wanted to know how to do something, I would simply find the person who knew how to do it, and I would have them share their step-by-step system on the podcast. The plan was to then go one step further and get my team to turn those podcasts into documented systems.

Pretty cool idea, huh?

Can you guess who the first person I interviewed was?

That's right. I sat down with a podcast expert who could teach me everything about how to produce a podcast.

That very first podcast show covered creating, editing, launching and marketing a podcast. I then gave that interview to my team to document and turn into a system that we still use to this day.

As ideas go, it was pretty good – even if I do say so myself (you can listen to the podcast here: www.SYSTEMology.com/podcast).

The astute reader might have just picked up one of the secrets to this process …

The first secret: creating systems is a two-person job

The SYSTEMology method of creating and documenting systems is very similar to my podcast idea. One person shares their knowledge (the knowledgeable worker) and another documents it (your 'systems champion').

This change, while small in principle, is huge in terms of getting the job done. If you try to get one person to do both parts of the task (explaining *and* documenting), I can guarantee you'll hit resistance. But if you make this a two-person job where you just record what the person is already doing, while they're doing it, and then assign someone else to document the system, you absolutely change the game!

You can then maximise the accuracy of the process by getting the knowledgeable worker to review and edit the created documentation.

Most people, if they have a choice, much prefer to edit something that already exists, rather than having to try to create something from a blank page. Get 'version one' of a system done by someone else (someone who likes writing these sorts of documents) and you'll find it infinitely easier to get the knowledgeable worker to review it. Give it a try.

Like many things in business, fighting strong resistance head-on is rarely the best way forward. Play to your team's strengths and do everything in your power to make it easier for them to do their best work.

Your systems champion

Continuing with this train of thought, is there anyone currently on your team who loves creating systems and processes? They might not have consciously realised it, but you can typically spot these people because they're known for being extremely organised, detail-oriented people. They're the kind of people who enjoy creating to-do lists and organising projects, and get great satisfaction in seeing things run smoothly.

It's worth identifying these people early and getting them involved in the SYSTEMology process. Whether it's to help with interviewing the knowledgeable workers, creating the documentation or just overseeing the process, they will play a key role in ensuring you get the results you're looking for. You always want to play to people's strengths, so make sure you get this book into the hands of the team members who can make this happen.

I recall a great example of finding a systems champion when I did some work for a company called Portavac, which cleans residential and commercial roofing gutters. One of the first things they did was identify their systems champion even before we even started work together. Kane was a curious, give-anything-a-go twenty-year-old who worked in their head office.

Over the course of a few months, he worked closely with me in applying SYSTEMology. He helped connect me with the right team members, attended all of my sessions with the team and even conducted some of the recordings himself. He even, on more than one occasion, literally grabbed a camera and went out into the field to capture different parts of their business process. He then shared those recordings with our team and helped with the documentation.

It produced some great results, and what I loved most about it was that it ensured they had someone who understood the whole methodology inside their business – someone who could keep driving the process forward well after we finished our engagement.

It really can be that simple. And I love this example because it highlights the fact that you don't need special training (beyond reading this book) to be a systems champion. The right person will just 'get' this stuff and they'll make your job easier.

If you don't think you have that person in your team just yet, that's okay for now. But the sooner you can find someone to take ownership over this project, the better. You might even consider hiring a new person for this position.

I've had great success, for instance, with return-to-work mums and dads. Often you can hire great, highly skilled team members who aren't able to return to work full-time but could work part-time in your business.

They may have worked in corporate or larger companies and can bring a wealth of knowledge. Perhaps you find someone locally, give them this book and have them help you implement it within your business. This could easily start out as a 10–15 hour per week job over a 3–6 month period, and if they prove to be a good fit, you can offer them a more permanent position later.

Either way, once you identify your systems champion, this is the perfect time for the business owner to step out of the process and allow their team to begin building these processes without them. Let the systems champion drive things.

The second secret: the System for Creating Systems

If the first secret to systems extraction is that it's a two-person job, the second secret is that you need a 'System for Creating Systems'. It's a bit meta – having a system that outlines the system for documenting systems – but successfully wrap your head around this now and everything after this will run just that little bit smoother.

This system template will outline the structure all your systems will follow to ensure consistency. It will remind your team to keep things simple and make it easy for anyone to easily capture, document and share what they're doing.

I'll walk you through the process here in more detail, but you can also grab an easily shareable version of the system here: www.SYSTEMology.com/resources.

Okay, you have identified your Critical Client Flow (CCF). You've identified who in your team has the knowledge, and now we need to get it out of their heads. Let's jump right in. We'll start by documenting your first system.

Step #1: Identify the result you're looking to achieve with this system.

Pick one of the identified systems from the CCF to be your guinea pig. I suggest starting with something simple so you can become familiar with the process.

Alternatively, you can pick a system that solves a very specific problem you know your business is having right now. For example, if you're having troubles around the delivery of your product or service, focus on the onboarding and delivery systems. Having trouble selling? Create a system for your sales process.

Either way, stay within the bounds of the CCF and prioritise at your discretion.

For our example, we'll pick an easy-to-understand process – handling inbound enquiries via the phone or website. We'll name it something clear but descriptive: 'Handling an incoming enquiry'.

Step #2: Identify who produces the result.

You've already completed this step in the previous chapter, so this is easy enough. Look at your DRTC and see who is marked as the knowledgeable worker of the system – the knowledgeable worker who knows HOW to do the job for which you're creating a system. We'll extract the system from them and then aim to bring everyone else up to that standard.

Step #3: Determine the capture method.

What will be the most effective way to capture the person who is sharing their knowledge?

Most of the time this will be recording them doing the task, as they're doing it, using screen-recording software, a camera or your mobile phone. See www.SYSTEMology.com/resources for our current software recommendations.

For an office task, I'd suggest using screen-recording software; for an outside job that is very physical, get a GoPro camera or something similar. For a sales task, you might just use a Dictaphone app on your phone or a combination of methods.

Note: In situations where it's not possible to capture the actual event happening live, have the knowledgeable worker roleplay the process or take the systems champion through their process step-by-step. Always look for the method that creates the least friction or anxiety for the team members.

Step #4: Record the task being completed.

If you're lucky, your knowledgeable workers will immediately recognise the benefits of systemisation and will be fully on board with the process. Otherwise, it's well worth taking some time to prepare them before conducting your recording.

Start by explaining why this systemisation process is being carried out and frame it in terms of the benefit to the worker. For example, having their tasks systemised will ensure their work can be managed effectively while they're on vacation.

"You know how every time you go on vacation you come back to a mountain of work to catch up on? Or worse, while on vacation you still need to keep working to keep things moving? This will ensure we can get the team to manage things while you're away."

You should also make it clear that the heavy lifting – the documentation, uploading, tweaking, etc. – is going to be handled by someone else. All they really have to do is carry out the task and talk about it as they go along. We'll cover more tips on how to introduce SYSTEMology to your team in a later chapter.

Depending on the complexity of the task, it can be helpful to ask the worker to make a few bullet point notes before the recording, outlining some of the key steps. This pre-planning gives the worker the chance to think through a task that they may have been completing on autopilot for a long time.

You should also stress the point that we're not looking to have this system 'perfect' or fully optimised. While it's okay to make minor tweaks, you want to avoid trying to completely re-engineer things. Optimising comes later. At this stage, we're looking to keep things simple and just capture how things are currently done.

One final point to keep in mind is that not everyone will be comfortable being recorded, so a little preparation and scene-setting can go a long way to calm the nerves. If you have a systems champion, have them schedule times on the calendar for when these extractions will happen and have them conduct the team member's recording.

It's time to hit the 'record' button and let the knowledgeable worker do their thing. Remind them to describe everything they're doing as they're doing it and aim to capture every detail you can. This will make things much easier at documentation time.

By definition, this team member is a knowledgeable worker. They know how to complete this task and they're able to complete it to a great standard. So, don't worry about any mistakes or interruptions in the recording. If you break off or, worse, restart after every flub, the task will take forever.

If the knowledgeable worker messes up, get them to explain what went wrong and then just carry on. Mistakes can be edited out in post-production if required, but sometimes the errors can be instructive if it demonstrates how to recover from a mistake. Just keep rolling and capture everything as you go.

In circumstances where the tasks may be completed in stages or where it's not possible to go through from start to finish in one go, just capture it in pieces. Later you can decide if it's best to combine these or keep them as separate standalone systems.

The final result won't be great. The odd element might have been missed, the recording might look a bit amateurish and/or the worker might have gone slower than usual. None of that is important.

Remember that your first version is highly unlikely to be the final, definitive version. You'll get better as you go along, and every time you create a new iteration, your end result will get a little better, a little more efficient and a little more accurate.

The Kaizen philosophy is embedded deeply in the SYSTEMology method. The idea behind constant and never-ending improvement is that nothing is ever finished or considered perfect; there's always room for improvement. You must get comfortable with this idea and just get your version number one complete.

Step #5: Create a new system.

The first time you document a system, you need to decide where you're going to store it. Ideally, you might already have a file storage system or, better yet, systems management software that can easily be managed, edited and accessed by everyone in your business.

We'll cover this in more detail in the next chapter, but either way, my best advice is to always go with whatever makes things easiest for your team members. There is a trend for software that attempts to do a little bit of everything; in my experience, this tends to overcomplicate things by providing lots of bells and whistles, 99 per cent of which you probably won't use.

Assuming you have your database in place, ready to use, your systems champion should now have everything they need to create a system based on the material that's been extracted.

Get them to create folders in your systems management software based on the different business departments you identified earlier, such as Sales, Finance, Operations, etc. The systems champion can then store a new system in the appropriate folder.

This system document aims to have everything in one place so your systems champion can do their thing. Here are a few extra points of information you might consider adding to your document.

System title: This should be concise, but not at the expense of using the most appropriate and descriptive keywords. Thought should be given to the search terms that your team might use when trying to locate this system in the future. Also, consider creating a naming convention to ensure consistency.

System description: Again, this should be brief but clear. It should state what the system is about and what results or outcomes are expected from following it. I would suggest not more than a couple of paragraphs.

Relevant links: Add a link to the video recording of the task being completed and other files, templates and required resources.

Knowledgeable worker: It's a good idea to have this person noted in the system itself since typically this person becomes the primary point of contact for questions relating to the system.

Team members: Identify other team members (or at least one) who you'd like to also be able to carry out the task. These team members can act as the backup for this task if the knowledgeable worker is unavailable.

This last point is an important one that starts to remove key person dependency and creates business owner freedom. Remember that all tasks and roles should have more than one team member who's able to step in and complete those duties.

Having redundancy reduces team member anxiety around taking

leave, provides business owner confidence and gets you one step closer to complete business reliability.

Step #6: Create step-by-step documentation.

Remember the first secret of the extraction phase is to make it a two-person job: the person with the knowledge and the systems champion.

Have your systems champion watch the recording of the task being completed and get them to note down the steps carried out in a linear fashion. Literally, "Step 1: Do this. Step 2: Do that."

Each step should be as detailed as it needs to be, using sub-bullets and clarification comments as required. These steps should be typed directly into the main body of the system.

How do you know if the level of detail is correct? There is no perfect answer here and it's often dictated by the system itself and the skill level of the team members who will carry out the task. Low-skilled roles with higher turnover of staff may require very detailed instructions when compared to tasks completed by highly skilled, long-term members, which may require less.

That said, I'm not a big believer in hiring unskilled fifteen-year-olds to do all the tasks in your business for minimum wage (unless you sell hamburgers … then I'll grant you an exception). Don't create every system for the lowest common denominator.

Take Reed Hastings' (founder of Netflix) advice from the *Masters of Scale* podcast: "What we failed to understand is by dummy proofing all the systems that we would have a system where only dummies wanted to work there."

The goal is not to develop robots who mindlessly follow step-by-step instructions. We want to give smart people the instructions they need to deliver a great outcome. Keep it simple, with less detail than you think you need.

Remember, you will keep evolving your systems over time (we haven't even got to the optimisation stage yet).

A reader with some knowledge should be able to read the main headings for each step and, from this information, have a good idea of what needs to be done. They should then be able to read all the additional information described in each step and, with a little practice and guidance, be able to complete the task to a good standard.

In one of the later steps, we're actually going to put this to the test. But for now, the systems champion should be aware that this is the goal when creating the system. It needs to be specific, clear and detailed enough to allow the process to be followed without any gaps. It can also be really helpful to conclude the documentation with a few criteria that can be used to double-check the task has been successfully completed.

The systems champion should also be consistent in their approach. The text, the style of writing, the layout, even details such as whether the step number is indicated numerically (1, 2, 3, etc.) or alphabetically (one, two, three, etc.) should be uniform throughout.

The right person for this job will be fastidious about achieving this level of detail and consistency.

Finally, the system should conclude with a 'supporting notes' section, containing the source videos and audios, required templates and attachments, and any other relevant information.

Step #7: Review the system.

Once you have your first draft, it can be sent to the knowledgeable worker who originally recorded it. They're usually the best person to judge how it's coming along. However, rather than simply reading it, get them to follow through the steps when they next complete the task so they can compare it directly.

They should be looking for errors, critical omissions and anything they think might send someone off track. This feedback can be made either directly into the system or to the systems champion for them to update it. Go with whatever is easiest for the knowledgeable worker.

At this stage, the system should be good for review by another set of eyes. If the department head hasn't been involved in the creation of the system until now, get them to take a look. Remember that the knowledgeable worker is focused primarily on getting a specific job done, whereas upper management can view the system from the wider point of view of how it impacts the department and other areas of the business.

This is also where you may discover insight into how other areas of the business can be improved and/or where energies and resources are being wasted.

Discuss any suggested tweaks and additions with the knowledgeable worker and adjust the system with any agreed changes.

IMPORTANT NOTE: Avoid seeking perfection. A common mistake made at this point is to re-engineer processes, trying to get it 'just right'. Someone may want to add a range of extra steps to improve the system or even add the use of a new tool or piece of software. While minor tweaks are welcomed, and will often improve a system, I strongly recommend you avoid introducing major deviations from how things are currently being completed.

Trust me, you'll get significant wins simply by getting consistency across all your team as they follow the new systems developed by your knowledgeable workers. We will look for optimisation improvements further along in the process, but for now just capture what is currently being done. You'll thank me later.

Step #8: Have your team follow the system and cross-train other team members.

The final step in the process for your shiny new system is to use it in the real world. The original knowledgeable worker can continue to review and tweak it over the next few cycles of that task being completed and, once they feel good about the process, they can use it to train someone else. This step is going to expose any remaining weaknesses and confusions in the documented system.

Have another team member go through the task, watching the original video, reading the notes and then completing the task. They can refer back to the original knowledgeable worker, asking questions and seeking clarity where needed.

This gives the knowledgeable worker or systems champion another chance to further improve the system. Repeat this step as often as required until the tester is able to complete the task to a reasonable standard without any intervention or feedback required.

You should also view new hires as an opportunity to review every system related to that person's role. A fresh pair of eyes will often reveal new opportunities to improve and streamline things.

Flow charts come last

I see this all the time when people read a book on Six Sigma – they think every system must first be flow charted before it's improved. Maybe this is true for multinational corporations and/or companies with existing detailed documentation, but for small businesses this is overkill.

Flow charts are a graphical representation of systems depicting inputs, decision points and outputs. The problem is that these are usually created by a systems nerd using some fancy software that only they know how to use. And because no one else can figure it out, once they're created, they're rarely (if ever) updated.

Remember, you'll want to involve multiple team members and make things as easy as possible for them. Don't set them up for failure by creating flow charts that will be out of date in the blink of an eye. Save it until the end, once your system has been in action for some time and you've been through the final optimisation stage of SYSTEMology. At least by this point, your flow charts will be less likely to need updating.

The same can be said for using too many screenshots within your systems. Often, I see systems that include screenshots for every step in a process, and while that sounds good for clarity, in reality it's a nightmare to keep them updated. Software updates all the time, so don't set yourself up for failure. Take my advice and keep your screenshots to a minimum.

Refer to appendices 1.1 and 1.2 for a couple of examples of systems from our digital agency. Just keep in mind, I modified these for simplicity and clarity.

Set yourself up for success

Great job, you're all the way through documenting your first system! Keep working through the CCF to keep you on track and commit to documenting a minimum of two systems per week. You might consider prioritising which systems you create first by those that you know will solve problems you're already having within the business.

This stage of SYSTEMology (the extraction) is easily one of the largest with regards to the volume of work. It's how the sausages get made. Commit to the process and get a solid understanding of the System for Creating Systems because, if you can nail this one, everything else will become that much easier.

I've used this system countless times and it's proven to work for virtually any kind of system imaginable. If you ever feel stuck or you're not sure how to capture a particular process, remember to simplify. Make the system an overview system and document only the top-level steps. You can always circle back around and create more detailed instructions for each of those steps if required.

This often occurs when you get to the onboarding and delivery section of the CCF. There's a very real possibility that this could get quite complex – please resist this urge the first time around.

Just do whatever you need to do to keep the momentum going.

Ask yourself, "How can I ensure I keep moving forward through the extraction phase?" I know it's easy to prioritise other jobs within your business, so how could you reward, punish and/or create some accountability for yourself?

One of the best examples of accountability I remember was from a colleague who had just quit his day job to become an entrepreneur, working from home. But what he didn't anticipate was just how hard it was going to be to get out of bed each day without the pressure of having to be in the office by 9 am. He was fine once he was up, but actually rolling out of bed each morning became a constant battle.

So, he came up with this ingenious idea (his self-inflicted positive constraint) to park his car in a clearway zone out the front of his house. If he didn't get out of bed and move his car by 8 am he knew it would be towed away, and this completely eliminated any temptation to stay under the duvet. The price was just too high.

How can you create a little positive pressure to ensure you and your team get all the steps in your CCF documented within a set timeframe? Which do you think will work better – the carrot, the stick or a combination of both?

Make the commitment, do the work and reap the rewards.

Case Study — Oh Crap

Oh Crap, a compostable dog poop bag company, started in Bruce Hultgren's garage in 2014. His co-founder Henry Reith's smart marketing strategies quickly launched the new company. Soon after their bags hit the market, sales exploded. They went from selling a total of 200,000 initially to 6.3 million poo bags over just a couple of years. After one of their first large orders, Henry remembers walking into Bruce's home to find floor-to-ceiling stacks of boxes, filling the garage, kitchen, even his boy's room. It was a true "we're actually doing this" moment.

Oh Crap's marketing soon outpaced their capacity for output, and when order volume spiked, they had to turn off ads. Then there was also Bruce's yearly week-long vacation which brought the business to a complete halt – this only compounded the stress!

It was time to turn this side hustle into a serious business. They brought on full-time staff, including Henry's sister, who quit her job to join the new team. The start-and-stop style of business in their early days wouldn't cut it now that they had wages to pay.

Henry had been involved in several successful ventures in the past and knew from past failures that they needed systems.

When a colleague introduced Henry to SYSTEMology, he loved what it promised to do. Even better, the approach championed having someone other than the busy owner to create, record and implement systems.

So, after Henry recorded their first couple of systems, he appointed an internal systems champion. Today, she keeps everyone honest with their systems, continuously recording and re-evaluating essential procedures. Thanks to systems, they're able to stay ahead of the growth – not frantically clawing to stay on top.

Bruce and Henry have the time and mental space to dedicate to driving the vision, and Henry can put his marketing expertise towards more creative, expansive projects. For the first time, they have more resources than orders, and that's a great thing, because as they amp up their marketing efforts, Henry predicts that the business will double every few months thanks to their systems.

"Extract" action steps

- Using your Departments, Responsibilities & Team Chart (DRTC) as a guide, create a timeline and get to work extracting your systems. You can prioritise based on solving problems you know currently exist within the business.

- Download and follow the System for Creating Systems for each identified system from www.SYSTEMology. com/resources.

  ▸ Step #1: Identify the result you're looking to achieve with this system.

  ▸ Step #2: Identify who produces the result.

  ▸ Step #3: Determine the capture method.

  ▸ Step #4: Record the task being completed.

  ▸ Step #5: Create a new system.

  ▸ Step #6: Create step-by-step documentation.

  ▸ Step #7: Review the system.

  ▸ Step #8: Have your team follow the system and cross-train other team members.

- Identify how you will maintain momentum. Will you use rewards, punishments or both to keep your team on track?

Organise

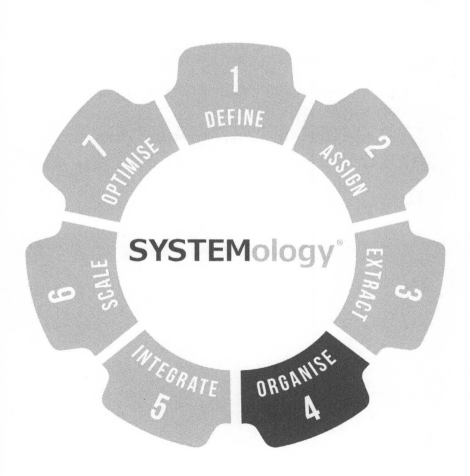

"Organise" Chapter Summary

The fourth stage in SYSTEMology is to organise the systems you have captured and implement the right technology to ensure your team actually follows them! You will discover how to overcome the dreaded "but I didn't know" and lay the foundations for high performance.

Highlights from this chapter include:

- *Why systems-centred businesses always get higher multiples and sell for top dollar.*

- *Why software will never be the 'holy grail' to business systemisation.*

- *Why it's critical to separate your systems documentation from your project management.*

- *What most people do wrong when they try to automate their workflows.*

Organise

MYTH

You need to invest in expensive and complex software.

SOME YEARS AGO, I WAS JOINT OWNER OF Planet 13, a rock 'n' roll-inspired clothing store. It was a fun but incredibly hard business to be involved in.

If you've ever operated a retail store, you'll know what I mean. Every month, even before you make a single sale, you've got to fork out for rent and wages. The overheads are sky-high, and you need to make a truckload of sales just to reach break-even.

Fortunately, I was working with some smart partners, and from day one our goal was more than just selling T-shirts. We were building the business with the view to sell it as a franchise. Our first store was the prototype – it was our opportunity to create, test and measure. We honed our business and developed a manual that detailed every step of how to run a successful store.

As we grew, we opened a second store, kept improving our systems and stepped out of working 'in' the store. We grew some more, hired staff, moved to our head office, built out our wholesaling arm and prepared to sell our first franchise.

I remember that part of the journey vividly because this was a key part of my role.

When it came time to sell the first franchise, I was selling our winning business model. I was selling our step-by-step systems, 'our way of doing things'. They weren't stored in fancy software, no wikis or cloud-based solutions – all of our systems were printed and stored in a simple binder. We had one manual for the team members in the store and one manual for the store owner. It was simple and it worked.

And you know what was most exciting? This was an asset we created out of thin air, and one that could then be sold many times over.

The money is in the systems

This burned a valuable lesson in my brain: extraordinary leverage is created any time you create something that can be sold more than once with minimal additional work.

It sounds obvious when I say it, but who wouldn't want to do work once and continue to get paid for it over and over?

I'll save the rest of the Planet 13 story for another day – I'll tell you about the shopping centre that tried to sabotage us by letting our competition open up three doors down from us, how we got caught in the global financial crisis and all the other sordid details … but for now, to cut a long story short, while Planet 13 isn't around to this day, the lessons I learnt in the school of hard knocks will stay with me for a lifetime.

This might be outside your comfort zone, and maybe you're not ready to hear it, but it is my belief that you should always be building your business with the idea that one day you will sell it. If you decide to sell all of it, part of it, or not at all, obviously that's up to you, but one thing is for sure: building it with the idea of eventually selling it ensures you build it on solid foundations.

Systems-run businesses are always worth more

You probably already intuitively know this to be true, but there are a range of reasons why. Most obviously this is because systems-run businesses function without key person dependency. They work without the business owner or any specific team member being essential to their operation. They're more efficient, more reliable and scalable.

Systems give the potential acquirer confidence that the business will continue to perform well after the sale. Your systems are the blueprint to your successfully run business, and they're worth their weight in gold. If you store your systems in the cloud, then they're worth their storage space in gold.

I personally believe that systems are the most important asset within your business. If you want to argue that the people are more important, I'll challenge your point, reminding you that, like it or not, people come and go.

No single employee, at any level, should be so critical to a business that they're irreplaceable. In fact, if you have someone in your business who IS irreplaceable, you have a big problem. Because what happens if that person gets sick, or someone in their family does, or, worse, they get hit by a bus? You're in trouble.

Systems, on the other hand, are the only assets that will stick with you through thick and thin, that can serve your business for decades and can even be replicated within new future ventures. They will be your library of solutions to common business problems, no matter what business you're working in or on.

I know you're already sold on the idea of systems, so no doubt I'm preaching to the converted, but the reason I'm labouring the point is to ensure we're both on the same page. The money is in your systems.

I know of one enterprising businessman who has built and sold his plumbing business twenty-one times to date. Each time he builds it quicker and better than the previous and sells it for higher and higher valuations. He starts by purchasing a failing plumbing business, then deploys his team and they install his systems to turn things around. At last count he sold his most recent company for tens of millions of dollars.

That's leverage and pure genius if you ask me.

Where do you store your most valuable asset?

Does your team know where to look to find your systems, or are they scattered across your shared drive, in folders on your team members' desktops or dumped in unorganised folders in your Dropbox account? You probably need a better plan than that, and that's what this chapter is all about. Let's look at how you will organise your systems and how you will create responsibility and accountability.

It's also time to break a few of the old misconceptions around what your systems manuals will look like.

The old ideas of printing out big, thick manuals and sitting them on a shelf to collect dust are obsolete. But similarly, the idea that you'll need complex enterprise-level software with built-in learning management systems (LMS) using SCORM is also flawed. All these thoughts are holding you back.

Start with simple

Yes, the times have moved on since my Planet 13 days and while the tools may have changed, simplicity has remained.

The fact is, if you can never master the simple, you'll never master the complex. So before looking at all the bells and whistles, automated solutions and new, shiny objects, let's agree to keep things simple.

There really are only two tools we need to get right.

1. You need a central location where all your business systems are stored. Getting this right gives you and your team certainty around how tasks are successfully completed.
2. You need a way to create accountability and hold your team to the standards you have de fined. This ensures you get the performance you desire.

Now, there's a chance you already have both these covered – it might just be you need a little tweaking to ensure you're using these tools correctly.

Without thinking about all of the tools and software you currently use (accounting, CRM, marketing automation, proposals, etc.), I just want to focus on two tools and what I believe you need to build a truly successful systems-centred business.

1. **Systems management software**
2. **Project management software**

Systems management software is where your systems are going to be stored so they can be easily accessed by you and your entire team. It will become the 'how-to' manual for everything in your business: every role, every task, documented and centrally stored.

Then there's project management software (sometimes referred to as task management or jobs management), which acts as an accountability and management tool. The goal of this software is to track all of your projects and ensure that every team member knows the tasks they should be working on and when they're due. This also gets all your team communication, relating to any project, out of your email and into a central location.

This is so important, let me say it more clearly. Stop using email to manage your jobs and stop your team from communicating via email. With email, tasks get forgotten, details get overlooked and due dates get missed. And to be clear, I don't hate email; it's an amazing tool, it's just horrible for project management.

When you stop and think about it for a moment, you already know this to be true. Have you ever tried to give someone a task via email only to have it forgotten 'til weeks later when you ask, "Hey, did you ever get XZY done?". The other person looks at you sheepishly and says, "Whoops, sorry, I forgot about that" or, worse, they have no idea what you're talking about.

This is all too common when you're trying to run projects via email. Communication is key – fix your team communications and you'll solve 80 per cent of your problems. Great project management software goes a long way to getting things on track.

The magic pair

Together, these two tools (systems management and project management software) allow tasks to be assigned with clear, easily accessible instructions that leave no room for confusion. Your team will be crystal clear on what needs to be done and where to look for the answers if they're not sure about something. This will dramatically improve your team's efficiency and eliminate excuses.

For micro-teams (or very small businesses) there's a chance you can get away with just the systems management software. However, as you grow past more than a few team members, you'll quickly realise it's one thing to have systems, but it's another getting your team to follow them.

If someone is new to a task, they'll most likely follow your system diligently on the first few occasions, but it won't be long before they feel comfortable enough that they'll stop referring to it. And that goes double for the knowledgeable workers who helped create the system. Moreover, it's also probably unrealistic – and unnecessary – to ask your employees to reread the entire system every time they complete their tasks.

That's where your project management software steps in. They may not always read the system, but you can insist that they check off the key steps in the process as they go along. The secret to ensuring your business develops a culture where systems are not just created, but actually used, is to introduce some level of accountability.

Use project management software to create milestones or checkpoints for the tasks that your team has to check off as they go along. The checkpoints for a task can be templated so, once set up, it's a snap to duplicate. And if you use the documented steps as a guide to creating checkpoints, the hard work has already been done. The end result is a uniformity of results that reduces errors and waste to a bare minimum.

Even better, for recovering micromanagers like myself, it's reassuring to know that, just because you're extracting yourself from your business, it doesn't mean you have to completely lose touch with what's happening on the frontline. When properly organised, you can use these tools to jump back into your business at any time and quickly get up to speed, even if your attention has been elsewhere for months.

A word of caution

Before I take you through the rest of this chapter, if you already have your systems management and project management software selected and they're working for you, there's no need to switch!

No one piece of software is going to magically solve all your problems and, ultimately, it doesn't matter so much which tools you use. The key is just to have *something* to meet each of these two key areas.

If your current software stack isn't working for you, you're going to need to weigh up your options, since there's a chance you're missing one or more of the key criteria I'm going to outline. You need to decide if it's worth the effort of moving and learning new software or if it's easier to find a workaround with your existing tools.

Either way, for the rest of this chapter, I'm going to assume you DON'T currently have a solution.

I've also separated the discussion of the criteria into two categories

– project management software and systems management software – because I would advise NOT combining the two. It's not that integrated solutions don't exist, it's that combining the two tends to come with compromises and unnecessary complexity.

I'll explain more as we get into things. In short, trust me, keep your systems management and your project management isolated and you'll reduce the likelihood of needing to switch software further down the road. You'll also set yourself up in the best possible position should you decide to sell your business at some point. A stitch in time here will save you nine.

Project management software

Let's start with project management software since there's more of a chance you already have something in place. Project management software is designed to cover the 'who does what, by when' aspect of task management.

There is a range of non-industry specific tools out there, including Asana, Basecamp, Trello, Podio, Teamwork, Monday and many more. And then there are the tools optimised for specific industries.

Be mindful of the latter group because these can sometimes be over-optimised for specific tasks at the expense of important departments within your business. For example, some software packages built for trades-based businesses focus exclusively on the scheduling and delivery side of your business. While this is important, it can be frustrating when you realise you need more than one platform to manage all the other departments within your business.

That said, depending on your business, its industry, the size of your team and what you do internally versus outsourcing, you may need one or more of these specialised platforms to function efficiently. For our purposes, project management software should be able to sit at the top level. It should cover all departments and set clear accountability for the actual doing of any work.

If you haven't yet found a project management tool, here are a few criteria to look out for:

- ☑ **Basic task creation**
- ☑ **Sub-task creation**
- ☑ **Task descriptions and links**
- ☑ **Task list templates or duplication**
- ☑ **Permission levels and project visibility**
- ☑ **Intuitive and easy to use**

Let's look at each of these in more detail.

☑ Basic task creation

At a minimum, your chosen software should allow you to:

- Create a task
- Assign the task to a team member
- Tag other team members who need to receive updates on the progress
- Set deadlines for when the task needs to be completed

To be honest, you'd be really hard-pressed to find a project management software that doesn't have these basic features. These are the fundamentals of good project management. But don't assume – check that these fundamentals are in place.

☑ Sub-task creation

Again, this is a pretty standard feature, but it's critical so be sure it's available. You need to be able to split individual tasks into a series of sub-tasks based on the required steps in the documented systems that you've created. These sub-tasks should also allow for assigning – it's this feature that will allow you to create true accountability in your team.

Sub-tasks are ticked off as the team member completes steps, which also allows you to ensure projects are progressing as planned and gives a place for comments and questions where they arise.

☑ **Task descriptions and links**

It's always helpful to be able to add notes and links directly into a task. Although it sounds obvious, some highly specialised software applications are so streamlined they don't allow for this.

I also consider this critical because one of the secrets to making your newly documented systems work is having them handy, right where the team member is getting information about the task they've been assigned. That is to say, you literally want to post the link to the step-by-step system at the point at which the task is assigned.

This is important for two reasons. First, it helps team members who are new to the task to quickly understand the steps required, and second, it clearly sets expectations. Your team will come to learn that by marking a task as complete, they are effectively agreeing that they have completed it to the standard outlined in the system.

This helps immensely with compliance and removes the "but I didn't know" excuse (more on this later).

☑ **Task list templates or duplication**

Given that the systems you create will typically be for tasks that are repeated often, it's a huge time-saver if you can set up new tasks from a template.

This feature typically works by allowing you to create a new task from a previously created template, containing the standard description, sub-tasks and links. Then it's just a case of modifying any specifics, such as the assigned team member and the deadlines.

Duplicating previously created or completed tasks is also fine, as long as the standard elements remain the same and the details can be modified as required.

☑ **Permission levels and project visibility**

Depending on the size of your business and the nature of your work, this might not be strictly necessary, but permission levels can be useful to limit what team members can and can't access.

A department head, for instance, might have the ability to create and assign tasks, whereas a regular team member might only be able to access and comment on tasks to which they've been assigned.

There are obvious security benefits to this feature, such as preventing individual team members from seeing what other colleagues are working on or keeping certain client details confidential. But this feature can also be used to make the software easier for your team to use. With restrictions, you can make it so team members only see the tasks that they've been assigned and literally nothing else. This gives clear focus.

☑ Intuitive and easy to use

Due to the wide variety of variables between companies, industries and situations, it's easy for project management software to quickly become overcomplicated. Just remember the key criteria I've outlined here and avoid chasing the latest and greatest shiny feature.

Unneeded features create complexity, complexity creates friction and friction lowers adoption.

There's nothing wrong with a broad feature set in itself, especially if you know that you'll have use for many of the extras. But an intuitive platform that can be mastered quickly is far more important.

Remember, it's going to be your whole team who uses this program, and not everyone may be tech-savvy. If the platform is awkward to use, difficult to learn or even just slow when navigating from one page to the next, it's only a matter of time before your team starts looking for ways to limit their need to use it.

You don't want to find yourself in a situation where people only log in to the project management software once per day, right before they finish for the day, just to tick off everything. This destroys the core benefit of project management software, which is to get your team to use the systems and to record their progress as they're doing their work.

Making the final decision

Before making the final decision on which project management software to use, put together a small focus group to test it out. Help them understand that the purpose of this platform is to make their job easier and get them to run a few projects and tasks through the platform, asking for their feedback.

Don't expect ringing endorsements from everyone, but listen to the feedback and carefully consider any criticisms before you make your choice.

A word on automation

I love automation as much as the next guy. Who wouldn't want the robots doing the work? But before you start setting up automatic triggers that fire once the previous step is complete or before you hook up Zapier to automatically fire a zap every time someone sneezes, let me suggest you try 'human automation' first. What's human automation, I hear you ask?

It's how Google approaches things – you know, only the biggest tech company in the world. It would be easy to think that Google would jump straight to automation when improving their search engine results. Of course they would rely on the machine to do all the heavy lifting when it comes to calculating things, right?

This isn't the case. Instead, Google's search team first identifies something they would like to improve. They then create a hypothesis and supporting documentation (a system) to test. Then the testing begins with thousands of manual testers, testing the results of the change. Google wants to fully test their hypothesis with human oversight before fully automating the system. This all takes place long before it is fully codified and then incorporated into the search algorithm.

So what's the lesson here? Think like Google. Do it manually first, perfect it and then automate it. This applies to all things in business! There's no point automating something 'til you're sure it's worth automating.

Systems management software

It's more common for a company to have project management software or job management software than systems management software, which speaks directly to the primary reason so many businesses have trouble with their systems and processes.

Where do you think most companies store their systems?

They're often scattered all over the place – they're on people's desktops, some are in Dropbox, others are in Google Drive or SharePoint, some are stored in Microsoft Word and others in text files. Some have wikis, WordPress plugins or even Google Sites.

The point is, if they're everywhere, that really means they're nowhere.

Systems management software solves this by creating a central location for all your systems and processes – it's the home of your most important business asset. Systems management software is purpose-built to make this whole process of business documentation easy and fun.

So how do you find a platform that's right for you? Here's my buying criteria.

- ☑ **Dedicated systems management software**
- ☑ **Attaching rich media**
- ☑ **Permission levels**
- ☑ **Sign off**
- ☑ **Intuitive and easy to use**

☑ **Dedicated systems management software**

My first tip is to avoid storing your systems in document management or file storage platforms (like Dropbox, Google Drive, Box, SharePoint, etc.); these quickly evolve into an unorganised mess of random folders, files and inconsistency.

Similarly, avoid wiki-style platforms that requires coding, HTML or special knowledge to use. Any platform with a steep learning curve or one that will primarily rely on only a handful of team members keeping it up to date is doomed to fail. To build a systems culture, you want your whole team to 'buy in' and use it.

You're looking for software that has been designed with the explicit purpose of creating, editing and managing your systems. If it handles your company policies and other training, that's a bonus. Yes, it's possible to hack other solutions together but this typically comes with compromises.

Remember, your systems management software will house the most important asset in your business.

☑ **Attaching rich media**

When it comes to building your systems, you need all associated resources in one place. From spreadsheets, to images, to audios, to email templates, to videos, to flowcharts, to any other file types that can't be added through regular text, it's best if you can embed those directly into your systems.

For example, your original extraction videos should be embedded directly to the relevant system. The software might require you to first upload the video to a sharing site, such as YouTube or Vimeo, before you can embed the video, and this is perfectly fine as long as it can be streamed directly from the systems documentation page without having to go to an external site or having to download the video.

The key is to have everything in one place.

☑ **Permission levels**

It's critical to have varying levels of access. Not all systems will be relevant or, for security reasons, need to be seen by everyone. You need to be able to assign systems to roles and then those roles to individuals, thereby limiting what they can and can't see and edit.

This particular feature also allows for quick and easy reassigning of roles and associated systems when team members are moving up or on.

This one is a biggie and often where non-dedicated platforms fall short.

☑ **Sign off**

Another handy feature and one of the secrets to compliance is to remove the possibility of a team member saying "I didn't know." Team members simply sign off and agree that they have read and understood a system. Be sure your systems management software has this feature.

☑ **Intuitive and easy to use**

Similar to my recommendation for your project management software, but perhaps even more critical here, is ease of use. Good systems management software should require almost zero staff training to get everyone up to speed. It should look and work in a way with which team members are already familiar.

Avoid excessive, often unnecessary, features that also overlap with the goal of your project management software. While automated workflows, active checklists, data collection, etc., all sound great, most of these features should live inside your project management software which manages the 'who does what, by when'.

Rather than making decisions based on "Oh, wouldn't that be cool" or "That looks like a great feature", always come back to the primary purpose of the tool.

Systems management software is where your systems are stored so they can be easily accessed by you and your entire team.

Project management software tracks all of your projects, ensuring that every team member knows what tasks they should be working on and when they're due.

Together, these two components are vital to your success in building a systems-centred business.

Software sorted – what's next?

Time to make these platforms your own...

Step #1: Customise your project management software.

I'm going to keep these next two steps super short since it'll be hard to give you direction other than the basics – this will depend heavily on your business, your team and the software you have selected.

That said, within your project management software, begin by setting up a workspace for each of your different departments identified (sales, marketing, operations, finance, human resources and management). Underneath the relevant departments, create tasks to match those identified in your Critical Client Flow and assign the knowledgeable workers related to them.

Step #2: Customise your systems management software.

Within your systems management platform, create folders (one for each of your identified departments, and sub-folders to help further organise things) and begin importing the systems you've created in early chapters. Assign those systems to their knowledgeable workers, grab the links to each system and post them in your project management software next to their corresponding tasks.

Don't worry if you can't visualise this just yet! It's always easier when you see how someone else has done it. Watch a short video showing you how your project management and systems management software work together – it's inside the resources here:

www.SYSTEMology.com/resources

Final word on software

To ensure this book stands the test of time, rather than recommending specific software we use by name, I decided to focus on the key considerations when making your decision. As I said right from the start, no software alone will be the silver bullet. See www.SYSTEMology.com/resources for current recommendations.

People are often drawn to bright, shiny objects, and while software may appear to be the missing piece that will solve all your systemisation woes, there's much more to it than a piece of software. Transforming your business into a systems-centred business needs the right software, training, management and culture.

As you progress through SYSTEMology, you will learn how to install all of these vital components.

Case Study   Mount Martha Preschool

Mount Martha Preschool is a highly regarded play-based non-profit preschool local to the coastal bushlands of Victoria. The school consistently meets – even exceeds – federal quality standards thanks, in part, to the committee of parents that leads it.

Soon after joining, committee member Daniel Power-Mirfin noticed that poor succession planning was causing stagnation and disorganisation in the decision-making process. When committee membership turned over, new members needed a month or more to get up to speed before they could even consider new policy initiatives. Talk about lost time!

As a supervisor in the mining industry by day, Daniel was no stranger to the importance of systems in highly regulated industries. That said, he also knew that the red tape many of these software solutions introduced would stop the initiative dead in its tracks for the preschool committee.

Daniel followed the SYSTEMology framework and moved from Word documents in Office 365 to an online systems management software, and this was a game changer. Finally, they had a solution that bridged the gap between systems, federal regulatory policies and training. With all the knowledge stored in one location, Daniel says, "future committees now have the tools to hit the ground running".

What's more, the school is better equipped to honour their values with transparency between committee departments, teachers and staff. It's amazing what a little reorganisation can do!

"Organise" action steps

- **See our current preferred platforms at www. SYSTEMology.com/resources.**

- **Identify what software you will use.**

  - Step #1: Customise your project management software.

  - Step #2: Customise your systems management software.

Integrate

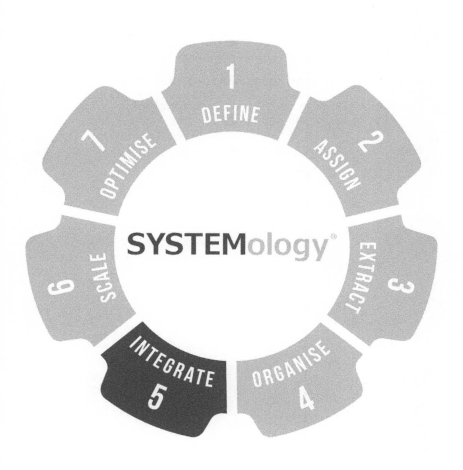

"Integrate" Chapter Summary

The fifth stage in SYSTEMology is to get the team to buy in to your new, systemised approach to business. Positioning the benefits of the new initiative in relation to the individual, rather than the company, is one of the secrets to making this work. Another is that people support what they help to create. Yes, change management is always easier said than done, but the good news is, we have a system for it.

Highlights from this chapter include:

- *How to get some perspective and identify your strengths and weaknesses.*

- *Why previous attempts to systemise may have failed you.*

- *What are the two most important roles in growing your business.*

- *How to deal with resistance from difficult team members who fail to follow your systems.*

Integrate

MYTH

**Even if you have systems in place,
your team won't follow them.**

O KAY! YOU HAVE YOUR CORE SYSTEMS documented and stored and your software all set up. Time for your business to magically start shooting out profits while your team diligently follows your systems.

Ha! You and I both know that's not going to happen. If it were that easy, everyone would be doing it! Having the systems in place is one thing; getting your team to follow them is another.

This trips up a lot of companies when it comes to systemisation. I hear the stories (and you've probably seen it firsthand) where a new initiative with the best of intentions gets put into place by a handful of key stakeholders, but within a few short weeks it's back to business as usual. People go back to doing things the way they've always been done.

This problem isn't isolated to the introduction of systems but extends to almost all areas of change within business.

Sadly, this also perpetuates the myth that, even if you have good systems in place, your team won't follow them anyway.

It's actually a perfectly reasonable assumption that if you were to just stop the SYSTEMology process at stage four, things aren't going to work for you. But, of course, you're not going to stop here. You're going to push on. You're determined.

Right?

I ask because, in many respects, this stage will be the most challenging part of the entire SYSTEMology process. It's manageable, and the process is proven, but you need to be ready to push everyone out of their comfort zone.

The key to ensuring that your business develops a culture where systems are not just created but actually used is persistence. You need to break through old habits, replace them with new ones and reach the point where your team knows, "This is just how we do things here."

You will face challenges, there will be resistance and at times you may even question if your team can make the transition. In these moments, keep the faith. Many companies have come before you and bridged this gap, and I have confidence you will too.

Also, take solace in knowing that your biggest challenge will come from existing team members who've been with you the longest and who might be set in their ways. For new team members, this way of work is all they know and very quickly they will discover if they're the right fit or not.

Identify your strengths and understand your flaws

I owned and worked in my digital agency for a little over a decade. In hindsight, it was a Frankenstein-style business since it was built up over time with a lot of crazy ideas, tools and team members all cobbled together. There was no strategic planning or structure.

We just kept marching in the direction of growth – more clients and more revenue. If problems came up, I solved them by hiring someone or purchasing a new piece of software. Everyone did their own thing and we pieced everything together as best as we could. It was functional but definitely not efficient.

It's funny how long it can take you to learn some things and then, once you learn them, how immediately obvious it becomes. You wonder why it took you so long to figure it out in the first place.

I always thought I was a good manager, but it wasn't 'til the last few years of my time in the agency that I realised my style was the reason we had stalled. Sure, I got on well with my team and people seemed to like working for me, but I was a micromanager. If I felt projects weren't progressing as I imagined they should, rather than coaching the team member or telling them that the work wasn't up to standard, I would often get in there and do it myself.

Now, there's nothing wrong with being a business owner who has a great relationship with their team. But if your business as a whole is going to grow and develop, some positive pressure needs to be applied. Otherwise, you're back to being the person who always steps in and saves the day.

To change your business culture, to build a business based on systems, it's going to take a firm hand and the willingness to hold people accountable. You don't need to be a tyrant – you're not going to whip your team members into shape – but you do need someone who is going to lead by example and who isn't afraid to tell people what needs to be done.

Here's the big question: is that you?

Are you the best person to lead the charge with this change? You need to be able to assess yourself honestly, push your ego out of the way and understand your flaws. If you need to, ask trusted colleagues for an honest assessment.

This goes beyond making the decision to let someone else take over and run with SYSTEMology – we've already established that many of the steps should be handled by someone who already loves systems and has extra capacity. This is about who should be managing the transformation of your company into a systems-centred business that is dedicated to following processes and procedure and rejects the ad hoc style of working.

Ultimately, this is the person who will run the daily operations of your business. For me, as hard as it was to admit, I wasn't the best person to do this.

The yin to my yang

Melissa, the person who eventually took my place running the agency, is my perfect counterbalance. She understands, values and is committed to building our systems-centred business. She's a better people manager than I was. She's well-liked by the team, but she doesn't need to be. This is not important to her.

This allows her to give someone clear instructions, step back and let them take responsibility for their work. She trusts the team to do their job. If a mistake gets made, she's created an environment where team members feel comfortable taking ownership, and she'll work with them to fix the issue.

She's also hard as nails and is comfortable pushing back on situations where the rules aren't followed. As hard as it might be to believe, she even does this with me as the business owner.

During my transition, I still had the bad habit of stepping in and throwing my weight around. I might, for instance, get tunnel vision and think of the project I was working on as being the most important. I would put pressure on a team member to get a job turned around quickly without considering their overall workload and how this might affect other clients' jobs.

This happened often enough that Melissa took the bold step of posting a message inside our project management software, advising everyone to ignore any 'Urgent' messages from me.

It was a gutsy move – no question about it. But she was well within her rights.

A few months earlier, Melissa and I had talked about how hard it was on the team when I would come up with a new idea every other day and then seemingly change directions at the drop of a hat. What was exhilarating for me was jarring for everyone else. They'd still all be coming to grips with my last innovation, and suddenly, I'd be talking about yanking them in a whole new direction.

Off the back of this meeting, we created a system for me to direct work through her. Talking to Melissa first gave me the opportunity to explore the new idea without distracting the rest of the business. She could help weigh up with the big picture in mind, make sure we didn't overcommit and ensure we worked on only the best ideas.

So, there we were. I'd put Melissa in charge, but I was undermining and sabotaging her work.

When I went to a team member directly with my 'Urgent' assignment, I was failing to follow the system that we'd already agreed to.

Her calling me out on this was a little embarrassing but it demonstrated to the team that we had a way of doing things and no one was above the law. As you can imagine, it didn't take long to get me back in line.

These days, if I have something that I feel is urgent, I can still take it to Melissa and we figure out how to fit it in with everything else that's happening. Sometimes it'll be a case of Melissa saying, "Yes, we can do it, but at the cost of THIS or THAT – is that acceptable?"

It can be pretty scary as a business owner to have someone else in the business challenging your direction, but I actually believe it's required to grow to the next level. Without it, you'll eventually slip back into your old role of trying to do it all and have it all.

The leader and the manager

The two roles I'm really speaking to here are the roles of a leader and a manager. The truth is you need both.

The leader is quite often the founder and/or business owner. They're the problem-solver, quick with ideas and full of drive, passion and creativity. They're great at starting businesses, inspiring others and powering them forward through a mixture of hard work, quick wits and raw instincts. Their blessings are a double-edged sword, though; with too many 'good ideas', they often find themselves moving onto the next thing before they finish the last.

Compare that to the manager, who gets things done. They're highly detail-oriented and quite often the glue for the organisation that holds everyone together. They ensure everyone marches to the same drum and is accountable for their work. Most importantly, they are very process-driven and have the patience to see a job through to the end.

Yes, of course you can grow a business without one or the other, but if you have both, and they can learn to work well together, that's a recipe for explosive growth.

This might also give you some insight into why you may have tried to systemise your business in the past but failed. It's entirely possible that, as the business owner, you're a great leader in desperate need of a manager to lock things down.

The leader and manager partnership is one of those things that might be new to you. But once you're aware of it, you'll start to see examples of it in many great growing companies.

For instance, did you know that Walt Disney had a brother called Roy?

Seriously, Google it. I'm not making this up.

Walt was the visionary leader who everyone knew and loved. Roy was the guy behind the scenes, making things happen.

Or how about Henry Ford, the founder of the Ford Motor Company? We all know about Henry Ford, right? But what about James Couzens, his general manager, who handled the day-to-day operations?

Another one?

How about Ray Kroc? You know, the McDonald's guy! He took

a hamburger restaurant in Illinois, USA and turned it into the most successful franchise of all time. But he couldn't have done it without the assistance of his right-hand man and manager, Fred Turner.

Often, we don't hear about the managers because it's the visionary leaders who are usually the public face of the company; they enjoy, at least to some degree, being in the limelight. Managers may not mind some attention, but they don't tend to seek it out. They're too focused on driving every resource and team member to achieve the company mission.

Are you a leader or a manager?

If you're a start-up founder, there's a good chance you're the leader. Some people are a mixture of both roles, but very rarely can you find someone who can do both roles well at the same time.

So, who's the manager in your business?

You might be lucky and discover that you already know someone, maybe even someone within your existing business, who would be well-suited for this role.

Or maybe you have to hire this person. If this is the case, you don't have to rush your search, but I want to plant this seed. At some point, to truly step out of the business, you will need someone to step in and run things. You need to figure out what your strengths and weaknesses are, and then use this knowledge to help you find a person (or persons) who will complement you.

For now, as it relates to SYSTEMology, it's okay to proceed as long as you have someone who you've identified as the systems champion (discussed in 'Step Three: Extract'). At a minimum, this person will take ownership over the process and dramatically increase the success of this new initiative.

Let's dig a little deeper into how you will roll SYSTEMology out within your team. As I noted at the start of the book, I advise reading through the entire book at least once before following the action steps since some of the later chapters (like this one) will help you with earlier ones.

Depending on where you are in the process, you may have already introduced your department heads and knowledgeable workers to SYSTEMology and that's okay! The steps I am about to cover speak more broadly to how to introduce things to the team.

Obviously, everyone's circumstances are different, so you will need to adjust accordingly.

Step #1: Identify who's leading the charge.

It should go without saying that you need to convey your determined, unwavering commitment to making this most important change to your business. But you also need to determine who's going to be the best person to lead the charge when it comes to implementation.

If you're a leader personality, this definitely won't be the first time you've introduced a 'revolutionary' new idea to your team. So, you only have yourself to blame if some of your team members secretly roll their eyes and wonder if this is an idea that will stick or will be replaced by something new in a few months.

If you have a manager on your team, they will be the perfect choice. Otherwise, a department head or senior team member may be a good fit.

Identify this person upfront, give them this book and ensure you're both on the same page.

Step #2: Know your selling points.

By this stage, you can probably already reel off many of the key benefits of SYSTEMology and talk about them with enthusiasm. But I want to give you a few more that you might not have thought about. I want you to have a strong, long list of reasons you can use to help build some positive pressure.

You don't need to memorise this list of benefits (unless you really want to). But having them handy, along with a deep understanding of the results SYSTEMology can produce, will go a long way to strengthening your resolve.

This list, while not exhaustive, hits the main points and can be roughly grouped into benefits for team members and benefits to the overall success of the business.

Team member benefits
- Fewer errors and less wasted effort
- Improved employee onboarding
- Reduced micromanagement
- Eliminate single-person dependency
- Identify and fill gaps in competency and capability
- Empower team members to develop and improve

Business benefits
- Duplicate best practices
- Improve results for clients
- Free up time for strategy and product refinement
- Scale up for profitable expansion
- Make the business more attractive to future buyers or investors
- Run efficiently even in the absence of founders or managers

Step #3: Introduce SYSTEMology to your team.

Getting all of your team, at all levels, into one room to announce your plan to systemise is perfectly fine if this is the norm for your business. But it shouldn't be your first venture into the subject.

Your partners, managers and team members are all going to have different questions and concerns, so it makes sense to bring each group into the conversation separately.

A top-down approach is the most logical route. Get your partners onboard by sharing with them the business benefits. Then move on to your department heads, knowledgeable workers and team members using the team member benefits.

Remember, everyone is different, so you want to frame things with their perspectives in mind. Ideally, you don't want to move onto the next group of people until the current group shares your level of commitment.

Here's the thing... change is scary for many people, and the topic of systems also has baggage around it. People have preconceived notions on what this will or won't mean to them and their work. Many times, they have reached their conclusions without fully testing their assumptions. We have addressed many of the biggest myths as you work through this book, but there will no doubt be others.

It may be unrealistic to think you can get complete buy-in from everybody on the first attempt. Some people will 'get it' and embrace it while others may take more time before they fully commit.

Just remember, if your team members feel like SYSTEMology is going to make their job harder or they can't see the clear benefits to their situation, you'll get pushback. Put yourself in their shoes. Think of their current problems and how SYSTEMology can help to solve them.

For example, you might say something like …

"You know what it's like when you go on vacation (or you're sick) and you come back to find all your work has piled up. Your inbox and voicemails are full, you have one million tasks that have been waiting on you and now you need to work double-time to get back on top. You spend the next three weeks trying to get things back on track for the one week you took off. Well, we're looking to document some of your key systems so it's easier for other team members to step in and help out when you're on leave."

Or maybe it's something more aspirational.

"We would love to move you into a more senior position but to do this we'll need to delegate some of your current duties. By creating some step-by-step systems it's going to be infinitely easier to elevate your position."

See how those two reasons might appeal to different people?

Walk them through the Critical Client Flow and the Departments, Responsibilities & Team Chart. Ask for their help in refining and tweaking those documents. Have them as part of the process. People are much more likely to stick with something they have played a part in creating.

Remember to set the stage and address any concerns about the process being time-consuming or difficult. Tell them about your plan to make this a two-person job, where someone else will be doing the documentation. All you need is their help to capture what they're already doing. Easy!

Remember, people are great at reading energy, so be sure to introduce this with excitement and focus on the opportunities this will create for everyone.

Step #4: Start the extraction process.

With your key players onboard, your systems champion selected and your knowledgeable workers ready to go, it's time to start the extraction process. Work through your CCF using the System for Creating Systems and let your systems champion do the heavy lifting.

That is to say, focus on making it as easy as possible for your knowledgeable workers.

Step #5: Introduce your software.

If you already use project management or job-assigning software, simply add the links to your systems (stored within your systems management software) to your project templates.

Remember, the goal with your systems management software is to have all your documented systems already there, easily accessible at the point at which they're needed.

Combine this with your project management software and you have full accountability for the completion of the task to the required standard.

Note: Don't expect every team member to open a system every time they're completing a task – especially the more experienced ones. That's okay; just having them mark a task as complete is a step on the right path. It's the job of their manager to then ensure it's completed to the required standard.

Step #6: Manage via the systems.

Once all the big rocks are in place, you must start to make your systems central to the way you do things.

For example, you need to train your team to always look to the system first. If they want to know how to do something, if they have a challenge, if they've got a question, whatever it is … their first port of call should be to review the relevant systems and/or search your systems management software.

Systems empower your team and it gives them a resource to get their questions answered without judgement. All too often, new team members fail to ask questions when they're not clear on a task because they're worried about whether that would make them look silly. A systems database empowers your team to be self-sufficient.

I have been as guilty as anyone of slipping back into old habits when we first started this management style. Especially when it came to responding to questions from my team! My instinct was to try to solve all the problems myself. I'd answer any question on the spot because it was easy, fast and I liked being helpful. But the truth is, all I was doing was training my team to come to me whenever they had a problem.

Melissa eventually coached this out of me (another reminder that you need a manager with the courage to stand up to you). The fact was, managing the team this way didn't help me or the team member in the long term. These days, when someone comes to me with a question, the first thing we do is open our systems management software and look to see if the answer is in there.

This makes me happy since I still get to be helpful, but more importantly it trains the team member to look for answers themselves before asking for help. If they can't find the answer, this is an opportunity to improve a system and/or create a new one.

This environment also makes it safe for team members to alert their supervisors when something goes wrong. Individuals no longer feel like they're expected to take the blame. It's always the fault of the system, assuming everyone has followed the established processes – the focus is on improving the flaw in the system rather than blaming an individual.

It's just a better way for everyone to work.

Of course, if a problem is caused by a team member who failed to follow the outlined steps, their supervisor has a clear path to a resolution. They can start by reminding the team member that by marking a task as completed, they are confirming it has been completed to the outlined standard in the system.

If the standard isn't met, it's a sign that the team member needs further training and/or a reminder to follow the documentation.

This will result in one of two scenarios. Either the team member will get into shape or they won't. If they don't, we need to uncover why and get to the heart of the resistance.

Step #7: Identify resistance and meet it head-on.

Yes, there's a good chance that through this process you will meet some resistance.

To be clear, I'm not talking about the people who push back, grumble or struggle to change the way things are done. Be persistent and patient with these individuals, make sure they're held accountable for their progress and these bumps will smooth themselves out.

I want to address how to deal with people who either outright refuse to participate, procrastinate and/or sabotage to the point where it amounts to the same thing. These are the people who create tension in the workplace and who risk undermining your efforts.

There are many reasons why people resist change, but some of the more common reasons include:

- Some people may hide behind the idea that no one else in the business knows how to do their job. They feel this gives them added job security. The idea that their knowledge and experience is going to be documented could be unsettling because it implies that they might eventually be considered replaceable.

- Other people have learned how to make their workload appear heavier than it actually is, to the point where they fear that documenting their work might uncover how little they actually do on a day-to-day basis.
- Still others have been with the company for so long and are so used to doing things a certain way, they feel like they have the freedom to dig their heels in and resist change. These can be the trickiest to tackle.

Let's not wait for these problem personnel to show themselves. Decide in advance how to deal with these problems depending on your preferred management style. For instance, you might decide on a three-stage approach that starts with discussion, moves on to disciplinary action and concludes with termination.

Always start by putting yourself in the team member's shoes, trying to understand their motivations and helping them to see why change is necessary. It's good practice to try a few different approaches. You might find the solution is as simple as linking people's success with SYSTEMology to their performance reviews and bonuses.

However you decide to approach this step, it needs to be clear to everyone that becoming accountable for their work is not optional. Time will be given for everyone to adjust and learn the new procedures, but opting out is not on the table.

If this step is making it sound like SYSTEMology is going to result in a round of mass terminations, remember that this is about preparing for the problem. If you take a benefit-led approach to presenting your new approach, most, if not all, of your team members will join with you.

As much as anything, this step is about ensuring you're committed to following through, even if difficulties arise.

Don't lose sight of the ultimate goal of SYSTEMology: complete business reliability.

Step #8: Build a systems-thinking culture.

The term 'culture' often feels airy-fairy or, at best, something only big companies should worry about. The truth is, it's more important than you realise. Your business' culture is one of the biggest influences on how your team members behave.

Perhaps it's because your culture attracts similar team members; maybe it's because people look to the actions of those around them to decide what's acceptable and what's not; maybe it's just a reflection of the health of your business.

I'm no expert on culture building, but I do know a thing or two about embedding systems-thinking into a business. The good news is, you're already well on your way.

Putting systems front and centre when you assign tasks, focusing on the way you create accountability and managing your team via systems all play an important role in building the culture you need to make this work. I also suggest getting clear on the qualities your team members need to have to succeed within your business and building that into your recruitment process.

Imagine building a business where you attract the right team members to you and repel those who aren't a good fit. It's entirely possible and, as you would expect, it's a process. The point is, you need to deliberately cultivate this sort of environment. This doesn't happen by chance. In the next chapter, we'll discuss your hiring, onboarding and management systems.

You want team members who are primed for systems-thinking and you need to spot these qualities upfront. It's also important to stress that you're not looking for robots who mindlessly follow instructions. Quite the opposite – you want smart team members who think! Systems are simply documented ways to handle recurring tasks within your company. Systems allows team members to focus on areas where they can add the most value.

Heck, we think it's so important that we added it to our company values!

"Systems-Thinking. We always seek out and create systems-centred solutions for any recurring tasks and challenges."

For you to achieve complete business reliability, you must become a systems-centred business. This isn't just about having documented systems or the software tools to store them. Your team, at their core, needs to develop a systems-thinking mindset.

Not everyone is a systems person

Pinned to the wall of my bedroom was a piece of paper known only as: The Sheet.

Created by my father, The Sheet was his attempt to gamify his children's life. Based on the mission-critical systems that he believed were essential for having a rich, meaningful existence, it offered points for completing various tasks, such as washing the car, getting on well with my brother, going to bed on time and so on.

The number of points that I earned would determine how much pocket money I received at the end of the week.

But this was more than just a simple checklist of chores that converted into our allowance. The Sheet was an elaborate system that rewarded consistent behaviour. Points accumulated over time and exceeding certain limits would result in the award of additional cash bonuses.

The idea was that The Sheet would encourage and build positive and responsible habits that would become deeply ingrained over a long period of time (see appendix 2).

I just wanted the money!

So, I figured out how to play the game. I worked out which jobs provided the most points for the least amount of effort and made sure I exceeded 300 points a week for successive weeks to activate the cash bonuses.

I cracked the system so completely that my dad had to change the rules. It was either that or get a second job to cover my massively inflated pocket money.

I was eight years old.

As much as I loved a system that was fun to follow and with which I could maximise my results and pocket money, my brother hated it in equal measure. He loathed the sheet, and if he ever scored points it was usually by accident.

He simply had a different model of the world to me, and it taught me a valuable lesson. Some people just won't follow your systems no matter what you do. As they say, you can lead a horse to water, but you can't make them drink.

There's nothing wrong with this, it's neither good nor bad, it just is. There's no point in getting upset by this or trying to force someone into doing something they don't want to do. You have decided to build your business a certain way and if someone identifies themselves as someone who doesn't resonate with this approach, the sooner you discover this the better.

There will be times when you need to make difficult decisions. Just remember, it's worth making those tough choices sooner rather than later because you'll be one step closer to building a team who loves this new way of doing things.

Case Study   Inception Websites

Inception Websites is a comprehensive online marketing agency that primarily serves chiropractors. As former chiropractors themselves, Aimee and Mike Hamilton founded the company when colleagues started asking questions about their own thriving practice. Other chiropractors wanted their secret to lead generation.

So, Inception Websites was born. Through a combination of quality outputs and smart marketing, the business quickly picked up speed. They soon had the curse that every entrepreneur thinks they want: more business than they could handle.

In the beginning, Mike and Aimee saw new client growth of 3–4 per month, but as their business grew, that number spiked up to thirty. The first couple of times that they reached thirty new clients in a month, they found themselves backed up by several months. So, advertising paused until they caught up on the work.

"We would be losing business just because we couldn't handle the customers properly." If they wanted the business to grow, with the same exceptional client experience they prided themselves on, something needed to change.

They discovered me through my early digital marketing videos, followed the rabbit hole and progressed to SYSTEMology. It was time to systemise their operations.

We started by documenting their Critical Client Flow. Then they used this to train new hires. The result? For the first time, they were able to keep ads running for an entire year. No starting and stopping, no letting down clients, no value surges or dips.

And the best bit, Mike found: "When we have time to be

creative, we grow ten times faster than we do when we're stuck in the everyday jobs." Growth brings with it its own challenges but now, with the company culture of systems-thinking, the solutions are swift and efficient.

"Integrate" action steps

- ▶ Step #1: Identify who's leading the charge.

- ▶ Step #2: Know your selling points.

- ▶ Step #3: Introduce SYSTEMology to your team.

- ▶ Step #4: Start the extraction process.

- ▶ Step #5: Introduce your software.

- ▶ Step #6: Manage via the systems.

- ▶ Step #7: Identify resistance and meet it head-on.

- ▶ Step #8: Build a systems-thinking culture.

Scale

"Scale" Chapter Summary

The sixth stage in SYSTEMology is to extract and organise the systems required to scale your business. Your business as a system is only as strong as its weakest link, therefore, it's vital to document all areas of your business. The goal is to get your business to a point where there is no single-person dependency and you're well-positioned to leverage every opportunity that comes your way.

Highlights from this chapter include:

- *Why the secret to scaling is directly tied to your capacity to deliver.*

- *How a solid recruitment and onboarding process attracts superstar systems thinkers.*

- *The one exception to the rule that you should capture your current best practice.*

- *Why sending your best team members on vacation is one of the smartest things you can do.*

Scale

Systemisation destroys creativity.

T HE MYTH THAT SYSTEMISATION DESTROYS creativity stems from the idea that systems turn everyone into robots, incapable of original thought. This is just flat out wrong. In reality, systems create space, and space opens doors to creativity, inspiration and opportunity.

Did you know that many of the greatest and most creative minds in history leveraged the power of systems to increase their decision-making power? Einstein, Jobs, Zuckerberg and Obama, for instance, all claimed to have multiple versions of the same outfit – effectively a uniform – that they'd wear each day so they wouldn't have to dedicate any brain power to thinking about getting dressed in the morning.

Essentially, they had a system for clothes selection.

They believed this simple system gave them an extra level of efficiency that created space in their brain for more important thoughts and decisions. This is just one simple example, but we can only imagine how many other simple systems they created with the same objective, with each system, building on the last, saving a little extra time and creating a little more efficiency. Imagine taking those savings and compounding them over a week, a month, a year or even a lifetime! How much extra space have they created with just a few simple systems?

I'm not suggesting this is something you should specifically imitate, but it illustrates the power of systems to nurture creativity, rather than stifle it. Moreover, you'll come to learn that your biggest opportunities in business will present themselves when you're thinking creatively AND have space to take advantage of them.

Business owners must learn to step out of the day-to-day operations, to systemise routine tasks and work on the highest leverage activities that only they can move forward.

So, what systems will YOU need to scale your business?

Obviously, and like all things in business, there's no one-size-fits-all magical system that will turn your business into the next Amazon, Google or Netflix. The strategies vary widely from industry to industry and so too will your circumstances and opportunities.

The key is to understand where you are and where you want to get to – remember back to the four stages of business systemisation.

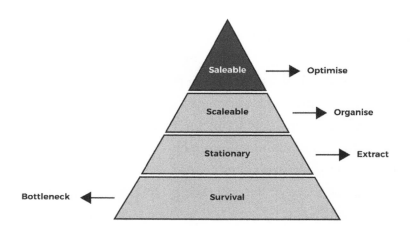

This chapter focuses on moving you from stationary to scalable. Remember, these stages are linear and you need to have completed the previous steps to succeed at the next stage.

Therefore, at the very least, your CCF – those core systems – must already be documented before you begin this chapter. The CCF focuses on the specific objective of having the business make money without being dependent on any one specific team member, so be sure that these systems are up and running.

They don't have to be perfect, but as long as you have something in place, you're ready to consider the other mission-critical systems required to keep your business functioning.

As we work through the other departments within your business, there's a good chance you will realise you haven't given much thought to these other areas. That's okay; like everything in business it's a constant work in progress. If we can at the very least identify the holes, it will become infinitely easier to fix them.

So where do you start? Just as before, we'll identify the critical systems, select your knowledgeable workers and begin the extraction process. Download the worksheet at www.SYSTEMology.com/resources and follow the steps.

Step #1: Identify your systems for growth.

Look at your Departments, Responsibilities & Team Chart (DRTC) and notice the departments with few or no systems identified.

We're going to focus on critical systems from three particular departments (finance, human resources and management). We want to identify the next 15–20 systems needed for documentation. In this step, we only need to identify them. These will be listed on a piece of paper in bullet point form.

I'll walk you through those three departments; however, if there are other departments that are of particular relevance to your business, it's okay to add them in here too.

Finance department

Unless there's a pressing need somewhere else in the business, I like to start with your finance systems. The good news is, 'finance people' (bookkeepers, accountants and CFOs) love systems and they're usually very happy to (with a little guidance) break everything down into their component parts. The finance department is made up of a set of repeatable systems that occur on a consistent and regular basis.

Invoices need to be issued, wages need to be paid, bank accounts need to be reconciled and tax obligations need to be met ... and all of that needs to happen on a day in and day out basis.

Ask the department head what needs to happen for the finance department to function at a bare minimum. Focus only on tasks you are already doing, not those you would like to do, and, if it helps, it's okay to brainstorm as many ideas as you can to start. We can apply the 80/20 rule after.

I like to take a blank piece of paper and list out the headings daily, weekly, fortnightly, monthly, quarterly and annually. Under each heading I then list each system that comes to mind as bullet points under those time periods.

Then, once you have a good fifteen or more systems, take out a highlighter and identify the critical 5–8 systems that are core repeatable tasks. This obviously won't cover everything and that's okay. We just want a starting point.

Remember, your business is already a going concern and tasks will continue to be completed as they have always done. We're just looking for a small collection of tasks that occur on a regular basis and that are critical to the operation of the finance department.

Here's an example of what the final output may look like:

Weekly
- Issuing invoices (already identified in the CCF)
- Paying expenses
- Reconciling accounts

Fortnightly
- Payroll

Monthly
- Preparing and sharing cash flow and profit and loss statements

Annually
- Conducting end-of-year financial analysis

That's it! Your goal here is to simply create a list of 5–8 systems.

Note: If you're outsourcing much of your financial department to a bookkeeper and/or accountant, focus on the areas you have control over and where you're required to prepare information for your partners. Yes, longer term it's still a good idea to develop complete systems for this department, but your current goal is to first free up your team's time and increase their efficiency.

Let's move to the next department ...

Human resources department

As far as systems go, hiring, onboarding and managing your team are among the most important areas of business to get right because they directly impact *who* you hire and, ultimately, how well they will fit within your company.

We've already squashed the myth that your team won't follow systems. 'A-players' love to know what's expected of them and how they can succeed in a role. This is why it's so important to get your core systems documented and set the standards early. Establish, right from the start, "This is the way we do things here," and you'll be well on your way.

How well you do this is one of the biggest determining factors to your success in building a systems-centred business. Magic happens when you define a clear way of doing things and have the right people executing them to those standards.

The good news is that there's a system to attract the right team members, introduce them to your way of doing things and how you manage them on a daily, weekly, quarterly and annual basis.

Similar to what you just did in the finance department, loop in any relevant team members and brainstorm ideas. On a blank piece of paper, build a list of all those processes relevant to the human resources department.

IMPORTANT NOTE: If you don't have a current way of doing things in the human resources department, don't stress. I will make a unique exception in the next step. That is, you don't have to only focus on tasks you are currently doing. List all the systems that come to mind, including those you would like to have implemented.

Then, just as before, highlight only 5–8 of those systems that are core for this department.

These may include:

- Hiring (definitely include this one in your list)
- Onboarding (and this one too!)
- Leave requests
- Daily team member routines
- Annual team member reviews

Like all things, add or remove items as needed and add to the list you made for your finance department.

Management department

The final department we need to look at is management. This covers how you choose the strategic direction for the business, how you review performance, set goals and ensure you're on track. This can be quite a deep topic and there's lots to cover depending on the size and complexity of your business. We're going to keep it simple, though.

I'm going to steer you to identify systems around your meeting cycles and the agendas for those meetings. Consistent meetings with specific agendas are the secret to great management. We just need to make sure you're not having meetings for meetings' sake and ensure every meeting is designed to deliver a specific outcome.

It might be a daily team meeting, a weekly sales meeting, a monthly meeting with your bookkeeper and a quarterly or annual planning session – it doesn't matter the exact rhythm as long as you have something in place. And remember, you're not looking to re-engineer parts of your business just yet (with the exception of a few of those HR systems). For now, capture what you're currently doing – our goal is to make it consistent.

SYSTEMology always begins by capturing the way things are, right now; if you spot gaps in your current way of doing things, just note it, create a placeholder and come back to it later once we start optimisation.

Also, if you follow the meeting rhythm from books such as *Scaling Up*, *Traction*, *The 12 Week Year*, etc., you can simply list these!

Include any key team members in this process and brainstorm your current meeting cycles. List them all, then highlight the most critical 5–8 ones. Here's an example to get you started:

- Daily team meeting to keep everyone on track
- Weekly sales meeting
- Monthly meeting with the bookkeeper
- Quarterly planning meeting
- Annual strategy and planning meeting

Once you have these added to your list, you should have a total list of between 15–20 mission-critical systems split between your finance, human resources and management departments.

Step #2: Assign, extract and organise.

You've identified and listed 15–20 department-critical systems. You may have already realised we can now follow the same process we used to capture the systems from the CCF (see 'Step Three: Extract').

Simply populate your spreadsheet with the system name, add a description and list the knowledgeable worker. Then, using the System for Creating Systems, begin the extraction process.

Remember, it's a two-person job – the knowledgeable worker and the systems champion. In situations where the system seems too complex, start with an overview-style system first.

Lastly, save the new systems in your systems management software and add a link to the relevant systems wherever the task is assigned for completion.

Sounds simple, right?

It is, but please don't confuse simple with easy. Simple is uncomplicated; easy is comfortable. This process is simple but not necessarily easy. There is work involved here and that takes focus and discipline to complete. But trust me, the rewards are worth it.

As before, I advise against heavily re-engineering your systems the first time you capture them. Avoid trying to capture things as you would like them to be. It's okay to make minor tweaks, but tremendous wins can be gained by simply modelling what your best team members are already doing and then bringing everyone else up to that standard. Most small businesses lack consistency, and that causes more issues than you realise.

The final stage of SYSTEMology is all about optimisation, so we'll get there!

Work through the list of 15–20 systems identified in the previous step and begin the extraction process.

Capture what you're currently doing, except ...

When it comes to the rule of capturing what you're currently doing, depending on how you're currently doing things, you may need to make an exception with two of your human resources systems: hiring and onboarding.

Building a great team doesn't happen by chance and it's critical you hire only the best. Trust me, put in the work here and you will be handsomely rewarded.

These systems will form part of your new team members' first experience and it's vital you bake your systemised approach to business into these systems.

If you already have some systems in place, they may need some modification, or you may need to create entirely new systems – it just depends on your situation. I'm not suggesting you need anything overly complex; it might only involve a few modifications to what you're already doing. The goal is just to ensure you demonstrate to prospective and new team members that you run a systems-centred business.

A handful of small tweaks can have a big impact.

For example, a great modification would be to include links in your position descriptions to some of the systems related to the role you're recruiting for. You might even consider adding them to your job ads.

In this way, you're effectively saying, upfront, "We have a way of doing things here and you need to be comfortable working in this way."

You may want to go the extra mile and consider adding 'systems-thinking' as a core value to your company values list. I touched on that in the previous chapter.

Either way, let's look at the first of the two systems you must have in place: your recruitment system and your onboarding system.

Recruitment system

The truth is, if you don't have anything currently in place, just having a recruitment system will go a long way to helping you attract the right team members. Average team members like to sneak in under the radar; 'A-players' love a system where they can demonstrate their skills and stand out from the crowd.

---

1. Write and post the job ad
- Write the position description and person required.
- Write the job advertisement.
- Create a questionnaire that interested applicants can complete to apply.
- Post the job ad on popular recruitment websites.

2. Shortlist, trial task, CV and cover letter
- Create a shortlist of applicants who have responded and filled out the questionnaire.
- Create a suitable trial task to gauge the skill level of the applicants.
- Send a trial task to the shortlisted applicants.

- Shortlist applications again.
- Ask applicants for a CV and cover letter.
- Send successful submissions to team members for review.

3. One-on-one interview

- Create a shortlist of the candidates you want to interview.
- Schedule interviews and advise those who have been unsuccessful.
- Create interview questions and then conduct interviews.

4. Hire

- Contact relevant referees.
- Select the successful candidate and make a formal offer.
- Once the successful candidate accepts, advise other unsuccessful candidates that had made it to this final stage.
- Agree to a commencement date/time with the successful candidate.

Obviously, this is just an overview-style system to demonstrate the key steps. Over time you may add supporting documents and/or subsystems that detail everything from example job ads through to the questions you ask in your interview.

When the time is right, I recommend you go deeper into learning about recruitment systems. There are many great books written on the topic (most notably *Topgrading* by Brad Smart). We've also had numerous recruitment systems shared on our podcast at www.SYSTEMology. com/podcast.

Remember, the first version of any system is almost always the worst it will ever be. Every iteration improves the system and the results.

Team member onboarding system

The second system I advise you to engineer is your team member onboarding process. That is, the steps new team members follow to be welcomed into your team. This is another critical system because it helps to set the right standards. Just like your recruitment system, I strongly suggest working elements of your systems-centred approach into your onboarding.

Here are a few ideas to get you started:

- Welcome video from founder (include company history and values)
- Training on your core tools and software (email, systems management and project management)
- Explanation of the CCF and where the new team member fits within the business
- Review of the core systems relevant to their role
- Sharing of daily routine
- Completion of relevant forms

Lastly, give all new team members a copy of this book and say, "This is the way we do things here and we need your help to build the business following this blueprint." In fact, why not buy a copy of this book for every one of your existing employees? Buy them two if you like.

In all seriousness, however you want to approach this, I can't understate the benefits of investing time and effort into correctly onboarding your team members. This will play a major part in their success.

These two areas – recruitment and onboarding – are the only exceptions where immediate modifications are beneficial and recommended. Continue working through all the systems you have identified.

The objective of this chapter is to extract and organise the 15–20 critical department systems. Your systems champion should drive this, creating a realistic timeline and supporting your team members at each step.

Step #3: Identify key team member's critical systems.

Clearly there will be some lag time between completing the previous step and starting this one, but I want to get you thinking about it. Ultimately, we're working towards an elimination of key person dependency with respect to the daily operations of the business and sending your team members on vacation is the only real test for this.

Technically, you can carry out the same test by firing people, but vacations are much more fun!

It's natural to feel nervous about this step but you can calm your anxieties by reviewing the work you've already completed. Many of the systems that are critical to key roles will have already been captured through the earlier steps. And while there are literally hundreds of systems that can be documented, typically there are only a good few handfuls that really matter and even fewer that need detailed documentation.

This step ensures nothing absolutely critical has slipped through the cracks.

It can be helpful to think of the systems you're capturing in batches.

Batch 1: the CCF

Batch 2: critical department systems

Batch 3: key team member systems (this is the one we're about to complete)

Separating your work into batches in this manner forces you to remain focused, accountable and makes it easier to stick to a timeline, so don't move to this new batch until you've completed the previous ones.

Start by prioritising the key roles within your business. Typically, I like to start with business owners, department heads and key team members that deliver parts of the CCF. Get a blank piece of paper and create headings for the names of your identified team members. Then, starting at the top, it's just a matter of chatting with each member and asking the question …

"If you were going to take a month-long vacation, to keep things moving, what tasks and responsibilities would we need to ensure we cover for you?"

Let them know you want them to be able to take a restful and enjoyable vacation knowing their key tasks are taken care of. Focus on recurring tasks critical to the core operations of the business and help them brainstorm all their ideas. Then, as before, grab a highlighter and identify the most critical 5–7 tasks per team member.

The steps are always the same for each batch: identifying, assigning, extracting and organising. Just limit yourself to 5–7 systems per team member and no more than five staff at a time.

Stay focused, get the work done and then celebrate by actually taking a vacation.

You've got this!

Step #4: Go on vacation.

It's time for a vacation. Not for everybody at once. Obviously. Start with the business owner and then move on to key team members. A little extra organisation may be required, but with your systems documented, organised and integrated with your project management software, it will be infinitely easier for you to assign tasks and ensure the business continues to operate smoothly.

The first time a team member takes leave, it's normal for at least a few things to go wrong. Don't worry, this is all part of the process. The whole point of sending people on vacation is to spot areas you missed or ones that can be strengthened.

Time to give yourself a pat on your back. You have done some tremendous work and you have significantly altered the trajectory of your business.

Problems become opportunities

The "Scale" chapter of SYSTEMology is not about creating opportunities; it's about preparing for them. It's about opening up the capacity and scalability of your business.

You have no way of knowing when opportunities are going to present themselves or exactly what form they will take, but this stage will help you to prepare for a wide range of possibilities. That's the best any business owner can do when planning and preparing for scale.

Perfection in this area isn't attainable because it would require infallible foresight. But you *can* stack the deck in your favour.

When you truly master SYSTEMology, you will begin to recognise every potential problem, and every potential problem will look like just another opportunity to create a useful system.

Case Study   Den Lennie

Den Lennie is busting the myth that you can't systemise creativity. In his business mastermind program, he coaches small video production business owners to help them scale.

Ironically, he says, "The biggest problem I had in [my] business was actually me." He's a "creative at heart" and yet he felt scattered and distracted by a tangle of daily tasks that stifled creativity. It was inefficient at best. Making some strategic hires was the next step, but he needed to figure out how first.

In the past, he had this notion about hiring 'specialists'. He thought, *You just hire them and let them figure it out*. But that's not how it works. There's too much room for interpretation, and new hires will do what they *think* needs to be done. All new hires need guidance.

Like most of us, he started with project management software, but he soon realised that he needed something more than project management. He needed systems.

That's when he came upon my work and immediately began implementing the SYSTEMology approach. He realised that, for anyone to work effectively, they need a framework. SYSTEMology gave him the structure to refine his business' frameworks. Then he set a virtual assistant to building out his systems.

Systems streamlined that new hire guidance and coloured in all of the grey areas. Den found liberation in six short months, plus more revenue.

Now, through a partnership, he coaches his business clients to follow the SYSTEMology approach. The results have been stunning. One client completely removed themselves from day-to-day operations in only three months. They credit systemisation with the efficiency that led to their highest-revenue month so far.

Den insists that systems help to unlock the creative process. Frameworks give plenty of room for interpretation and creative latitude without bogging the creator down with the minutiae of routine or technical processes.

"Systems," he says, "really do set you free."

"Scale" action steps

► Step #1: Identify your systems for growth.

► Step #2: Assign, extract and organise.

► Step #3: Identify key team member's critical systems and assign, extract and organise these.

► Step #4: Go on vacation.

Optimise

"Optimise" Chapter Summary

The seventh stage in SYSTEMology involves creating a dashboard that gives you visibility into your business and then beginning the process of optimisation. We identify the problems, make system improvements and then monitor the results. When the team becomes unconsciously competent in this skill, it unlocks the door to complete business reliability.

Highlights from this chapter include:

- *Why trying to imitate McDonald's is hurting your systems development.*

- *Why watching too many metrics causes confusion and slows progress.*

- *How to make systems improvement simple, fun and automatic.*

- *The simple secret to accelerating your business optimisation.*

Optimise

You need to systemise like McDonald's.

THIS MYTH, MORE THAN ANY OF THE OTHERS, sets you up for failure. Think of McDonald's as an elite athlete who's competing at an Olympic level in the sport of business systemisation. They're a lean, mean, systemised machine. They've been training their whole life and they've won numerous gold medals.

Now, compare that to you and your business … How long have you been training for? How do your systems and processes look?

Compared to them, we all look like couch potatoes.

It would never make sense for you to try to replicate the results of McDonald's by trying to follow their current habits, diet and exercise regimen. It sounds silly, but it's not uncommon for someone to get bitten by the systemisation bug and think they need their systems to be at McDonald's level before they start using them.

They start split-testing the equivalent of "Would you like fries with that?" or seeing how the colour of team members' shirts affects sales. And they do all this before they even have a baseline in place.

Like it or not, it just isn't possible to create Olympic-level systems on your first go – it takes hard work and consistency over a long period of time. But, in truth, you don't NEED perfect systems to deliver a great result, and it probably doesn't even make sense for you to systemise like a global fast food chain.

Don't get me wrong, there are great lessons to be learned from McDonald's. But remember the four stages of business systemisation from my introduction? If you try to jump from survival to saleable in one giant, pole vault-style leap, you're going to do your business an injury.

Let's not forget that McDonald's, in its current guise, is the result of six decades of development. If you get the chance, watch the movie *The Founder* – the story of Ray Kroc's efforts to turn the original McDonald's restaurant into a franchise. When Ray arrives on the scene, the McDonald brothers have already created a restaurant that functions as a well-oiled machine, and the movie only provides a glimpse into the years of hard work that went into reaching that point.

Before I saw this movie (warning – minor spoilers ahead), I didn't even realise that the McDonald brothers had already tried and failed to franchise their business. It took a lot of persuasion on Ray's part to convince them to let him have a crack at it. And while he eventually succeeded – obviously – there were a lot of problems and headaches along the way. The whole project would have crashed and burned if Ray hadn't … well, if you haven't seen the movie, I don't want to completely ruin it for you.

My point is that the McDonald's system was far from perfect when they started. It took years of optimisation to reach near perfection. It's good to dream big, but when you translate that into action, start by systemising based on where you are, not where you'd like to be.

Optimisation, tweaking and testing your way to a better business is useless – even counterproductive – if you haven't first established a solid baseline. One of the core principles in SYSTEMology is to first capture what you're already doing. That means if you're still getting your systems together, now is not the time to start optimisation.

It's entirely possible that your business structure is already pretty advanced and you've already carried out the earlier steps in one form or another. And that's okay too. Everyone will go at their own pace. But don't try to mix up the order of the steps or work on more than one simultaneously.

You can't improve what you don't measure

There are many reasons each step is ordered and prescribed in the order they are. And there are reasons it's best to leave system optimisation until last.

Perfection, person dependency and time constraints all do their best to stop you from getting to this final stage. Moreover, it's not possible to begin the process of optimisation 'til you have consistency in your work, making it possible to measure your outputs. Which, in turn, gives you a baseline to work from.

The deeper you get into SYSTEMology, the more you'll recognise your business is simply one large system pieced together by a collection of smaller interconnected systems. Everything is connected and small tweaks in one area of your business can dramatically impact another.

For example, by tweaking who you're marketing to and how, you'll dramatically affect your sales. This can then alter your selling system, which can alter the experience of your product/service delivery. This, in turn, impacts the likelihood for repeat business.

Long story short, these are just some of the more obvious relationships. The fact is, it's all connected, and it's easy to miss these relationships unless you're watching for them.

Continuing from the last step in the previous chapter, you and your key team members have returned from your vacations only to discover plenty of problems that still need to be addressed.

Before you jump into creating your next batch of systems, you first need to create a measurement system. A solid measurement system will highlight the interconnected nature of your systems, improve your consistency and allow you to predictably improve performance.

Let's break this down into clear action steps and begin the process of optimisation.

Step #1: Create a CCF dashboard to measure performance.

A dashboard, in this context, is simply a document stored in a central location with all of your key numbers and metrics from across your business. This is updated regularly at predefined intervals.

You may or may not already have something like this in place, but either way, it's easy to overcomplicate this step. There are many data points that could be included, and you'll quickly find that collecting data isn't the problem …

Analysing and gaining valuable insights that inform your actions from the data collected is the real challenge.

So, what's the 80/20 here? Of the thousands of metrics you could put on your dashboard, what are the most important? What will give you the greatest insight to how your systems are performing? You'll be happy to know the answer is right under your nose!

Take out your CCF and look at the headings that run down the left-hand side:

- Attention
- Enquiry
- Sales
- Money
- Onboarding
- Delivery
- Repeat/referral

This linear process describes the flow your clients go through in your business, which makes it a great place to start measuring. Over time, you'll discover other metrics worth tracking, but for now let's start here.

You don't need to measure everything. In fact, focusing on too many numbers tends to do more harm than good. So, let me challenge you, even if you have a dashboard in your company, to simplify. Let's set the goal to identify 5–7 key metrics that measure the performance of your CCF.

I'm going to work from the default template, but you'll want to customise it to suit your unique CCF. Again, we just want to identify one metric for each stage and list them on a blank piece of paper.

Attention: The ideal scenario would be to track all the people who come into contact with your business, but if pooling together multiple data sources to get a blended number is going to represent a logistical challenge, start with something basic. This could be the number of visitors your website receives or the number of people who walk through your shop door.

Enquiry: Shall we use the number of new email enquiries received? The number of inbound calls? Perhaps the number of proposals sent out? Maybe we could blend those figures together... or maybe not. Just pick one, preferably the data that makes it easy for you to collect and calculate. For this example, I'm going to go with 'number of proposals issued'.

Sales: You probably sell a range of products with a range of price points, but let's start with the most obvious – how many sales did you make? Your bookkeeper or inventory program should be able to calculate this one with ease.

Money: What's the average price of the product or service that you sell? If you feel there's too much variation in that figure, use the average dollar price of the central product or service you used to create your CCF.

Onboarding and delivery: There is a range of metrics you could be monitoring here – production time, number of projects in active development, inventory turnover, etc. That said, I'm going to combine these together to find one metric that gives us a pulse on how we're doing – profit margin. Your bookkeeper or accountant should be able to calculate this for you in a heartbeat.

Repeat/referral: Maybe you use your net promoter score? Or, if you're in a business where you get repeat customers, how many times do your clients come back? If you're in the software business, what's your churn rate? If you sell coffins and there's not much repeat business, how many referrals do you get? This one might be a little harder to calculate with your current data set but, at the very least, it should get you asking the question, "How would I measure this?" For our example, I'm going to use 'the number of times our clients come back'.

When you've finished this exercise, you should have a list that looks something like this:

- Number of website visitors
- Number of proposals issued
- Number of sales made
- Average sale price
- Profit margin
- Number of times clients return

These metrics focus on key areas of the business AND they're easy to track. Best of all, these numbers probably already exist somewhere in your analytics, your CRM and/or your accounting software, so it's just a matter of pulling out the data.

Next, create a spreadsheet that lists all these metrics in one row and then use the column to identify the date ranges. Decide on the frequency in which you want to capture these numbers. I recommend calculating these figures, at a minimum, on a monthly basis. Weekly is probably better, but keep in mind that, once you start, you're committing to keep this updated. It's okay to make things easy for yourself in the beginning, and you can always build up to higher frequency intervals later on.

CCF Dashboard						
	January	February	March	April	May	June
Visitors						
Proposals						
Sales						
Average Sale Value						
Profit Margin						
Repeat / Referral						

It won't surprise you to learn that I recommend assigning the responsibility of populating this spreadsheet to someone other than the business owner. It's a simple system that can easily be assigned through your project management software and you can then add it in as an agenda item for one of your regular meetings.

Need a ready-made template? Head to www.SYSTEMology.com/resources.

You now have most of the big rocks in place to really take things to the next level. You have identified and documented your most critical business systems, created a dashboard and established your management meeting rhythm. The work is far from over, but with a continued focus on consistency and bringing everyone up to the standards you've created, you're on the track to complete business reliability.

It's time to discover who's committed to helping you achieve your vision, where the biggest problems within your business still exist and what it's going to take to get everyone working together to reach your goals.

Step #2: Spot the problems.

Most business owners are great at solving problems, it's just that many get stuck solving low-quality problems over and over again. One of the goals of SYSTEMology is to move the business owner up the problem-solving ladder and have them working on the biggest-leverage, highest-quality and most important problems of the moment.

When you have a clear system for problem-solving, having the business owners shift back into problem-solving mode is actually a great use of their talents. It's simply a matter of identifying problems as they arise, prioritising them and then looking for a systems-centred solution. This ensures you do the work once and solve problems forever.

At the end of the last chapter, I suggested sending some of your key team members on a vacation. If this is the first time you've done this, when they return, a few new problems will have appeared – it's inevitable. These problems could have been caused by holes in existing systems or areas not yet covered by your existing documented systems.

If it's a quick fix or tweak, empower team members to fix the problems in the moment. This could be as simple as adding a comment to notify the knowledgeable worker to review things.

For larger problems, it's a good idea to create a new section in your project management software. Label it 'Problems List' and teach your team, whenever they spot a larger problem that's related to a system (or lack of one), to record the details as a task in this section.

In the early days, this list will grow rapidly. Add it as an agenda item to review it within your monthly meeting. If you've identified your systems champion, have them own this. Allow them to work through the list, categorising the problems based on your business departments and then prioritising based on urgency and impact. The approach is always the same – work in small batches and then identify, assign, extract and organise your systems.

There is no exact formula for calculating the order of priority, but begin by ensuring key team members (in particular) can take leave and still have their core tasks move forward.

Over time, your list of problems will shrink and problems that once seemed frequent and never-ending will disappear. New problems will still crop up but they'll be high-quality problems that, when solved, create big wins.

The key is to ensure it's a part of your regular meeting agenda so the team is kept accountable, and it's consistently addressed and moved forward. Systems development is a bit like eating an elephant: you have to do it one bite at a time.

Step #3: Begin optimisation.

Can you believe we're into the final step of the final chapter and only NOW do you get to begin optimisation?

This is all a little tongue-in-cheek, since you're bound to have made improvements along your journey. By focusing your attention on areas within your business, you can't help but improve them.

But I've steered clear of this topic because my focus has always been to first provide you with a solid foundation of systems. Before making any big changes, you need to shift the culture within your company. You need to allow your team to develop consistency and get everyone focused on the right metrics. This is why so much of the focus to date has been on capturing what you're already doing, rather than completely re-engineering and optimising your business.

This will seem counterintuitive at times because it's entirely possible to create a system that very quickly becomes outdated. But stick with me here. We're making things easy for your team, and this is probably the first time you've actually started getting some real momentum around the development of systems within your business.

Remember, before we began, your business was already (mostly) working, and we've modelled these systems from what your best team members are doing. We're looking for consistency and aiming to bring all your team members to that level. It's also comforting to know your new systems are always the worst they're ever going to be the first time you create them.

And if that isn't enough, in circumstances where you know you're going to have to completely re-engineer something, you can keep your documentation light at first. A few videos and some bullet points are enough to get things started. Only once you have a baseline of systems can you create enough space for your team members to start doing their best work.

You've also created a healthy, robust work environment – one where problems are identified and added to a list for tweaks, improvements or a complete overhaul.

The art and skill of growing your business now is knowing which areas to focus on next. Monitor your numbers, listen to your team and let your business tell you what it needs.

Listen to your business

I remember a good example of this a few years back in my own business. During a finance meeting, we identified a problem with clients paying on time. The data we'd generated showed that some accounts were 120 days overdue, and yet we were still performing work for those clients.

Slow payments are often seen as just part of doing business and the way things work in our industry. However, because we had the data and the space to discuss the problem, we identified that this was hurting our cash flow and, more importantly, it was something we felt we could fix.

We looked for the easy option first and decided to try an automated solution. Our accounting software let us send automated emails to clients if payment wasn't received. We created three levels of emails:

Email 1: Your account is overdue.

Email 2: Your account is really overdue, and if the bill isn't settled we'll have to stop work.

Email 3: Your account is really, really overdue. We've stopped work.

We knew it would be clear, fairly quickly, whether or not it was effective.

The short story was, it wasn't.

There was a slight improvement, but it appeared that clients were ignoring the emails. We knew from previous experience that if we called or even sent a personal email to the client directly, we'd often get a response, but the automated solution wasn't working.

While we would have loved to solve the problem on the first go, often you have to have a few goes at it. It's just part of the process of finding a solution. We'd implemented our first idea, gathered the data and found the issue reappeared on our problems list.

In our next monthly meeting, someone floated the idea of taking payment upfront and using automatic billing. The idea was to get payments to arrive consistently, in advance and without any action required by our clients.

This would require a little more work than writing a few emails so we spent some time talking over the pros and cons. Would new clients agree to this or would our conversions suffer? How would our existing clients feel about making the switch to automatic billing?

Despite some reservations, we decided the potential benefits outweighed the downsides and we adjusted our invoicing process.

1. New clients would be advised that auto-billing was required and that work would not begin until the first payment was received.
2. Existing clients would be asked to switch to this new system.
3. If an existing client objected, they would be permitted to remain on an account system, with the understanding that if they were late with a payment they would subsequently be transferred to auto-billing.

We had a little bit of pushback, but nowhere near as much as we'd feared. And, as hoped, we saw an immediate improvement. Whereas before, clients could be three or even four months late, now payments were made in advance, on time, every time.

Naturally, because this was a new system, we continued watching our metrics. Even though it quickly appeared to be a winning solution, we needed to keep an eye out for any unexpected side effects and be ready to adjust accordingly.

The takeaway from this story is the beauty of having a simple system for problem-solving within your company.

- Step #1: Identify a problem and add it to the problems list.
- Step #2: Discuss, devise and deploy a solution.
- Step #3: Monitor and review the results.
- Step #4: If the solution doesn't deliver the expected results, go back to step #1. If the solution does work, document it and make it part of your new process.

It's obviously not a complicated system, but it's extremely effective once you make it part of the way you and your team work.

In the early days, it may feel a little like you're just going around and around on a merry-go-round, but don't despair – that isn't a bad thing. The goal is to reach a point where your core systems are solid and you go through a cycle of identifying problems, fixing them and moving on to the next one. Business is simply a game of problem-solving. Wax on, wax off.

The accelerated method of optimisation

You may recall earlier I mentioned the wisdom one of my mentors shared with me about hiring a coach, consultant or expert in their field of expertise to help create the systems.

While I caution against this in the early days, having worked your way through much of the SYSTEMology process, you're now extremely well-positioned to get the most value from working with consultants. You have a baseline and know your key metrics, so before any re-engineering or major changes take place you can identify your current performance.

This is the ideal scenario for any coach or consultant because you're giving them something to work from. The process is still the same – you share with them the problems you're experiencing, and they advise on a solution. The difference is you now have a system for implementing new changes swiftly and the mechanism for reviewing the results.

Working with an expert can be an extremely smart way to accelerate things. Keep thinking about your business as a collection of systems and you'll recognise that the more you focus on building up your database of systems, the more valuable it will become.

Which brings us back to the last of the four stages of business systemisation: saleable.

This is what you're working towards. You may not be ready to sell and you might decide you don't ever want to sell, but by building your business as though it *is* saleable, you'll open a world of opportunities you never knew existed.

Multi-award-winning doggy daycare centre diggiddydog-gydaycare manages canine activities, exercise programs, grooming programs and day spas. Owner and founder Jeanette Farren was responsible for creating the business vision and managing the team.

Running a doggy daycare was a demanding experience. There were multiple stakeholders to manage including the dogs, their owners and the team. Handling live animals also required high standards and attention to detail. After running the business for thirteen years, Jeanette felt it was time to exit the business.

From the beginning, she had plans to sell the business. And with a background in business management, she was well aware that the best way to get top dollar when selling a business is to have the entire operation documented and running like clockwork.

Two years before the sale, Jeannette started the process of systemisation.

"The first areas corporate buyers look at when valuing a business are its accounts and systems. The earlier people can educate themselves about systems, the better," says Jeanette.

While she had already been diligently documenting procedures, she started to uncover holes that were proving difficult to fill. At this point, she came across SYSTEMology and attended one of our live workshops.

"SYSTEMology gave me a lot of clarity and momentum to organise my systems," Jeanette recalls. She started the process by documenting her Critical Client Flow.

It took some hard work but Jeanette went from working crazy, full-time hours 'in' the business, to stepping out of daily operations and working 'on' the business. Towards the end of the process she stopped going into the office completely!

While her hours within the business decreased, her confidence around selling diggiddydoggydaycare for a great price increased.

"I knew that we had done everything and more for the business to be a really good proposition for buyers – especially corporate buyers. At the point of selling the business, we were running at full capacity, systems and processes were on point and financials were solid. This gave the buyers confidence that they could take this model and deploy it in other locations," says Jeanette.

All ended well for Jeanette. She was able to exit her business and command a high multiple of profits. The eventual buyer highly valued diggiddydoggydaycare's systems, and they played a huge role in the valuation.

Jeanette is currently travelling around Australia taking the time to think about her next endeavour. Well done, Jeanette, you're an inspiration to many.

"Optimise" action steps

- ► Step #1: Create a CCF dashboard to measure performance.
- ► Step #2: Spot the problems.
- ► Step #3: Begin optimisation.

Now is the time

C ONGRATULATIONS, YOU MADE IT TO THE END! We've covered an enormous amount of ground here so it's a good idea to stop, take a step back and look at the seven stages from a high level.

Most books in this genre use their closing chapter to remind their readers of all the benefits of what they've just read and why they should act on it right away.

But in this instance, that feels redundant.

In my experience, the vast majority of people that come to me to learn SYSTEMology do so not because they want to be convinced of the benefits of systemising their business, but because they're already sold on the idea and they need a plan to make it all happen.

I'm the first to admit that business systemisation is not an original idea. It's been around for decades. You may have even tried to systemise in the past but failed.

What you needed was a system for making it happen, and this is the gap that SYSTEMology fills. Every small business owner deserves to have a business with complete business reliability! This is the reason, I assume, why most people will pick up this book. And if you've read all the way through to this final chapter, you're likely already convinced of its merits.

The argument for systemisation is strong and when you walk through the process, it's almost impossible to deny. No, a desire to act is not your biggest obstacle to getting started ...

The obstacle is WHEN.

When will systemisation become your business' top priority?

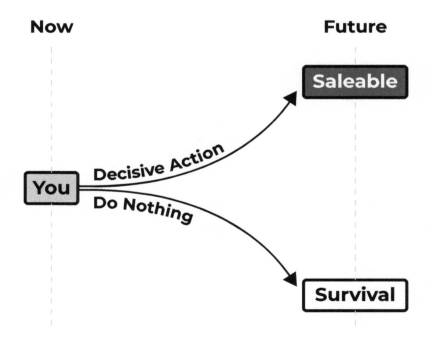

What we know for sure is that, as time passes, your future reality will happen automatically. The question is, what reality will you have?

The fact is, doing nothing costs you more than still being in the same place at some point in the future. The pathway to the future is never a straight line. It's a curve and it accelerates as time passes.

Do nothing and you will automatically drift further down. Moving up and riding that curve upwards takes clear, decisive action.

So, what options do you have?

If you lower the priority of systemisation for too long, jumping from survival to saleable is, at minimum, riskier, harder and more costly. And the reality is that, no matter how far away that upward curve feels right now, at this point in time it's as close as it's ever going to be.

Now is the time to make the jump!

Perhaps one of the best ways to move people from 'should' to 'must' is to focus purely on the bottom line. So, let's do that now.

How much is not systemising currently costing you?

While this is a tricky question to quantify exactly since the effects of systemisation are so far-reaching, don't worry – there's a calculator for that at www.SYSTEMology.com/resources.

The link above will take you to a financial calculator that provides a basic formula for calculating profit. This allows you to observe the effect small improvements in multiple areas can have on your business.

Small gains, when multiplied out, equal big wins on the bottom line.

Now I don't want to get too caught up in the maths, but I do want you to understand the numbers we'll be working with…

- Attention – how many people become aware of your business
- Enquiry – the percentage of people who become interested prospects

- Sales – the percentage of people who go on to make a purchase
- Money – the average price of the products or services you sell
- Repeat – the number of times a client comes back
- Margin – the profit you make after expenses

If these numbers look familiar, it's because they are derived from your CCF and CCF Dashboard. They're the key metrics from within your business and they're the numbers we're looking to improve as we install systems.

The question is, what size improvement do you think we can make by improving your systems? Do you think with some new marketing systems you could increase the number of people who learn and enquire about your business?

Do you think you could improve the number of sales your business makes by documenting what your best salesperson says and getting other team members to follow suit? Could you add a step to ensure your team always looks for other ways to help your client and upsell where it makes sense?

Do you think having a consistent way of onboarding clients and delivering work could reduce errors and increase efficiency?

Would all of these changes lead to your clients having a better experience that will, in turn, increase the likelihood they'll come back and refer new clients?

Do you think with a focus on your systems, capturing best practices, getting everyone following these new processes (and in some areas completely re-engineering your systems), would it be possible to get even just a 10 per cent improvement in each of these metrics?

Absolutely, and of course it's possible.

I've seen the introduction of systems skyrocket performance across the board far in excess of 10 per cent wins. But even with a conservative outlook, 10 per cent wins are well and truly achievable by installing good systems.

Now, here's the kicker. What do you think the impact would be to your business if you saw a 10 per cent gain in each of these numbers?

I'll give you a hint. It's not 10 per cent …

When you dig into the numbers, you'll discover that those 10 per cent wins compound each other and improve bottom-line profits by almost 80 per cent!

Let's look at an example …

- Attention – Imagine you get your advertising message in front of 100,000 people.
- Enquiries – 20 per cent of those convert from browser to enquirer (20,000 people).
- Sales – 25 per cent of those make a purchase (5000 sales).
- Money – Your average product price is $200.
- Repeat – Your clients purchase, on average, once per year.
- Margin – You make 25 per cent profit margin on your total sales.

To work out your profits, you multiply the sales, by money, by repeat, and by margin. In this example, that puts our bottom-line profit at $250,000.

Sales (5000) x Money ($200) x Repeat (1) = Revenue ($1,000,000)
Revenue x Margin (25%) = Profit ($250,000)

Now let's see what happens if you make a simple 10 per cent improvement in each metric across the board …

- Attention – You get your advertising message in front of 110,000 people.
- Enquiries – 22 per cent of those convert from browser to enquirer (24,200 people).
- Sales – 27.5 per cent of those people make a purchase (6,655 sales).
- Money – Your average product price has increased to $220.
- Repeat – Your clients now purchase, on average, 1.1 times per year – in other words, 1 in 10 clients makes a second purchase.

- Margin – You now make 27.5 per cent profit margin on your total sales.

Sales (6655) x Money ($220) x Repeat (1.1) = Revenue ($1,610,510)
Revenue x Margin (27.5%) = Profit ($442,890.25)

Can you see the power in this?

Simple, 10 per cent improvements in each metric, gained through deploying systems, increases the net profit from $250,000 to almost half a million!

That's an extra $190,000 in profit, from just a handful of 10 per cent wins.

And don't forget, these are conservative numbers. Get more than 10 per cent in just one or two areas, and the bottom-line profit soars. These are rough numbers and you'll no doubt have to make some guesstimates, but play around with the calculator and see what the impact could be to your business.

The point is to show the REAL cost of *not* installing systems. In this example, it is costing the business $190,000 not to take action. And that's just on the bottom line.

SYSTEMology delivers many unintended and welcome benefits, but if you want to get down to just the numbers, it's well worth finding out how much it's costing you not to systemise!

Be prepared for opportunities

I'll leave you with one final story. The story of how I wound up on a TEDxYouth stage in the Netherlands, giving a talk about – you guessed it – systems-thinking.

I wish I could give you a formula, like seek out speaking gigs on a specific subject, build a speaking portfolio, connect with a particular influential person and then you'll score a spot.

The sad news is, I don't have such a system.

The seed of the opportunity started early in my career when I was working in the stock market education field. I used to help people design trading systems. When I was starting out, I did a few speaking events and uploaded some of these to YouTube before moving onto other things. Cut to fifteen years later and a young guy on the board of TEDxYouth tells his father they're looking for an international speaker and asks him if he knows anyone who might be a good fit.

For reasons unknown, this guy's father remembers watching me on YouTube over a decade ago and suggests to his son that he reach out to me and see if I'd be interested.

Crazy, right?

I get an email out of the blue asking me if I'd like to be a TEDx speaker – which, for me, was one of the easier questions to answer – and six months later I'm on stage.

But here's the real reason I'm sharing this story ...

For the right person, speaking on a TEDx stage is a huge opportunity. It's instant recognition and it can do amazing things for your brand. But what most people don't realise is that there's a little more to it than just jumping on stage and talking for eighteen minutes.

The really tough part comes before the presentation.

Firstly, every TEDx talk has to be strictly non-commercial in nature. You can't pitch anything and there's no fee for appearing, so there's no direct benefit to your business.

You also have to cover your own travel expenses and accommodation, so there's a real cost for the privilege of speaking. And that's before we talk about the hundreds of hours you're going to spend preparing and practising the talk.

It's a pretty big commitment for no immediate commercial gain. But does that mean it isn't an opportunity worth pursuing? Of course not! Sometimes the best opportunities are those that most people are unwilling, or unable, to pursue.

Now, whether or not this sort of opportunity would make sense for you is irrelevant. The point is that opportunities present themselves all the time. Some you might decide not to pursue due to time or money deficiencies, while others you might miss because you don't have the headspace to see them.

Maybe there is a system for becoming a TEDx speaker, but if there is, I don't know it. My TEDx talk came about through yet another non-linear sequence of events that I couldn't replicate if I wanted to. Getting the opportunity was not something I had control over ...

But being prepared to take the opportunity when it presented itself was absolutely within my power.

The truth is, being ready to take advantage of opportunities as they present themselves will always get you the biggest wins. I suppose that's obvious by definition. Opportunity is 'a time or set of circumstances that makes it possible to do something'. Whether it's doing a TEDx talk in the Netherlands, working with Michael E. Gerber to launch his book or selling the MCG, Australia's most beloved sporting ground (you'll learn about the last one when you watch my TEDx talk) – you must be ready when the time comes.

Accordingly, if I were to wish anything for you, it's to have space in your own life to be able to take advantage of these non-linear opportunities when they present themselves.

I know if you're good at what you do, if you take the time to connect with others doing good work and you build a reputable business that genuinely solves your client's problems, opportunities are going to present themselves.

Sometimes when you least expect it.

I won't repeat my TEDx talk now (google it if you're curious), but a lot has happened since then and I have thought much about what I would say if I had the opportunity to share my thoughts on systems-thinking again.

If I had a do-over, I would discuss how creating systems is hard work and how you have to have the discipline to stick with it. It's mostly simple and straightforward, but it's far from easy.

I sometimes think that, in my talk, I made it all sound easier than it actually is.

But by now I think you know what's required.

Now is the time to get started. Make this happen. Not just for you, but for your team, for your family and for your community.

Stick to the path and you'll create results beyond your imagination.

Epilogue – Tragedy or opportunity

THERE'S NO OBVIOUS REASON I COULDN'T HAVE written this book a couple of years earlier.

For quite some time now, I've been honing the SYSTEMology approach and collecting numerous amazing stories of its application in a wide range of different businesses in disparate industries.

But for whatever reason I had a sense I wasn't quite ready.

Maybe I was scared I would fail? Maybe it was the universe waiting for the right moment? Maybe I was just busy and I find writing books a slow and painful process …

Whatever the reason, I'm glad I waited.

Because more recent case studies and my own personal experiences have illustrated the power of SYSTEMology beyond what I could have imagined even twelve months ago.

In fact, shortly after completing the SYSTEMology manuscript, I had an unexpected development that allowed me to produce an epilogue so perfect, you'd be forgiven for thinking that this was part of some master plan.

It started with a phone call …

Melissa (the incredible systems-oriented manager of my digital agency) contacted me to say she needed to head back to America to take care of some urgent family matters. Thanks to SYSTEMology, and Melissa's commitment to keeping these systems running when she took leave, the business didn't miss a beat.

The team stepped up and everything kept ticking along nicely.

But after a few weeks, Melissa returned and announced what at first was some devastating news: she planned to move back to America for personal reasons.

It was like a bombshell had hit. Melissa resigned.

So, what was I to do? Should I try to replace Melissa or take back management of the business myself?

Neither option was appealing. My passion for the agency died years ago, and with SYSTEMology at a critical point in its development, this wasn't the time for me to get pulled back into things.

Even if I did quickly find the right candidate, it would take my time to get them up to speed – time I felt I couldn't spare. Which really only left one alternative …

To sell the business.

The more I thought about it, the more it seemed like the right time for me to completely let go of the agency. The universe was giving me a friendly push out of the nest and letting me know it was now time to go all-in on SYSTEMology.

Remember, the four stages of business systemisation …

1. Survival
2. Stationary
3. Scalable
4. Saleable

To be the best example of what I teach and to take this business through to completion, selling the agency was the natural conclusion.

I set to work contacting a handful of people within my network. I had no interest in creating some kind of bidding war because my priority was finding someone I was confident would take good care of the agency. It wasn't just about leaving my years of hard work in someone else's hands; it was also my amazing team who were trusting me to find someone who would take good care of them.

Within a couple of weeks I had some good interest and two offers on the table.

Both interested parties had solid credentials, but in the end it was clear which person was the right choice. He was someone I had worked with previously, so he was familiar with and highly valued our systems-centred business. He had a great reputation in the industry and had plans to stay true to what we had built.

Even then, there was no need to rush. The potential buyer was appointed as acting CEO, giving us both a chance to do our due diligence. I got to see how he would handle the business, the team and the clients, and he got to look under the hood – so to speak – and examine the finances and the systems.

Once we were both ready to sign on the dotted line, we negotiated a fair sale (a high multiple of annual earnings), had the legals written up and the deal was done.

It was rewarding watching how smoothly everything came together.

Once the sale was completed, I asked the new owner what had attracted him to the business and helped him reach the final decision. Naturally, I was hoping that without prompting he'd refer to the systems that held the business together …

And I wasn't disappointed.

The financial performance of the business was important, of course, but seeing how comprehensively the systems were defined and recorded, resulting in a business that had been running independently for three years, gave him the confidence to take the helm.

I didn't sell the business just so I would have a nice epilogue for my book, but it just goes to show the importance of being prepared and building a business founded on solid systems. Without this, what options would I have had?

Sheesh, without systems, I wouldn't have had a saleable business. To quote an old Australian saying, "I would have been up sh!t creek without a paddle."

Fortunately, I *was* prepared. SYSTEMology gave me options. I now know with every fibre of my being that SYSTEMology transforms businesses from survival, to stationary, to scalable, to saleable.

And you know what? With that sale and my full focus now on SYSTEMology, I'm probably starting at the same place you are right now. We have successfully moved through the survival and stationary stages and *now* we're working our way through scalable on our way to saleable.

The steps that took Melbourne SEO Services through the entire life cycle are the same steps I'll be using again with my current business.

If that doesn't demonstrate the courage of my convictions, then nothing will.

What's next?

Anything's possible.

I can't wait to hear your story.

7 Myths of Business Systemisation – Summary

#1 **You will need to create hundreds of systems to systemise a business.**
This myth was busted in the first stage of SYSTEMology, *Define* - page 31.

#2 **The business owner is the only one who can create the systems.**
This myth was busted in the second stage of SYSTEMology, *Assign* - page 57.

#3 **Creating systems is time-consuming.**
This myth was busted in the third stage of SYSTEMology, *Extract* - page 75.

#4 **You need to invest in expensive and complex software.**
This myth was busted in the fourth stage of SYSTEMology, *Organise* - page 97.

#5 **Even if you have systems in place, your team won't follow them.**
This myth was busted in the fifth stage of SYSTEMology, *Integrate* - page 119.

#6 **Systemisation destroys creativity.**
This myth was busted in the sixth stage of SYSTEMology, *Scale* - page 141.

#7 **You need to systemise like McDonald's.**
This myth was busted in the seventh stage of SYSTEMology, *Optimise* - page 161.

Appendix

Appendix 1.1

Example system #1

This system is a more detailed 'how-to' document that provides the script to be used when an inbound call is picked up by one of the sales team. It's not a word-for-word script and isn't meant to demonstrate the world's best sales process, but rather give you the gist of how systems come together.

Title: Inbound sales phone call process

Knowledgeable worker: Melissa
Description: This system provides the script to be used when an inbound call is picked up by one of the sales team.

Step #1: Answer inbound call and clarify caller's position.

Answer the phone with the greeting, "Thanks for calling Melbourne SEO Services, <<Your Name>> speaking".

Oftentimes a caller will say something along the lines of, "I'm looking for help with my website" or "I want a quote for a new website". Once you know you're talking to a lead, follow the qualifying steps below.

1. **OPEN NOTEPAD: Open up a Word doc or notepad** right away so you can start taking notes as you progress with the conversation.

2. **CONTACT:** Make sure you get their **name, contact email and phone number** at this point and save it in your Word doc or notepad.

3. **SOURCE:** Thank them and then ask how they found us: **"Thanks for contacting us for help. Before I get started, can I just ask how you found us?"** Then take note.

4. **WEBSITE:** Then, if they didn't already specify, ask what their website URL is and how old it is: **"So I can take a quick peek, can you give me your website URL? And how old is the site?"**. Load the site in your web browser and, once it opens, acknowledge to them you're just taking a quick look.

   • **WEBSITE SIZE:** At the same time, open a new tab and enter in the URL field **site:<theirURL>** and press 'enter'. This will show you the **number of 'indexed' pages** for the site. We look at this right away because it helps determine how 'big' the website is, thus how much work there may be to do. Take note of the number of pages.

   • **WEBSITE CMS:** Next, load the site **https://whatcms.org/** and enter their URL so you can **ascertain what CMS** (content management system) they're using, if the site is WordPress (our preference) or something else. Take note of the CMS type based on the results.

5. **WHY?** Then, if they didn't already tell you, ask them what made them call: **"So I can get a better feel for how we can help, can I ask what made you call? Are you unhappy with your current provider? Change in traffic or conversions? Never done SEO?"**. Then take note of what they say.

6. **BUDGET:** Next, if they haven't already advised, ask them what their monthly online marketing budget is: **"So I can work out the best recommendation for you, do you have a marketing budget?"**. Take note of what they say.

Step #2: Quality lead scale and recommendations.

Use the lead scale and recommendations below as a way to work out what quality type a lead is. This will help you decide (1) what mode of contact we should use, (2) how quickly we should respond, and (3) what recommendations we should make.

- **"A" Quality:** has a WordPress site (OR if not on WordPress has an in-house or 'retainer' tech team) and has a marketing budget of **at least $XXX per month**. These lead types are "ready to go now", are not "rankings focused", are not a competitor to an existing client and are ideally on WordPress.

  Recommendation: These leads are perfect for the Starter Pack → Ongoing Services.

- **"B" Quality:** has a WordPress site (OR if not on WordPress either does the tech themselves or has a tech team) and has a marketing budget of **at least $XXX per month**.

  Recommendation: These leads are perfect for our Starter Pack offer → Monthly Web. Maintenance and/or Pack of 10 Hours.

- **"C" Quality:** has a WordPress site (OR if not on WordPress either does the tech themselves or has a tech team) and has a marketing budget of **at least $XXX per month**.

  Recommendation: These leads are best for Monthly Web Maintenance and/or Pack of 10 Hours.

- **"F" Quality:** has a WordPress site (OR if not on WordPress does the tech themselves) and has a marketing budget **under $XXX**

per month, OR is in **an industry which we don't work with.**
Recommendation: These leads are best for referring to our digital
training products or mailing list/free resources.

ACTION → Based on the answers this lead has given you, refer to the **Step
2: Quality Lead Scale and Recommendations** above, so you can make a
recommendation for them while on the phone. If they seem happy with
your recommendations, **send a post-chat email** using the appropriate
email template (if simple), or a proper proposal (if higher budget or more
complex) and send to them **within one business day.**

Step #3: Enter lead information into CRM.

All leads, irrespective of how they arrived, should be set up into CRM
with the appropriate data inputted then assigned to the relevant sales
team member.

- Once a lead is assigned to a sales team member, they will need to
  make contact with the lead (if they haven't already) and log that
  'activity' in our CRM (e.g. phone chat, email, etc.) along with any
  relevant notes or attachments (e.g. proposal).
- The sales team member's calendar and CRM need to be synced.
- Immediately after the activity is logged, the sales team member must
  set up another activity to remind themselves of the next follow-up
  with that lead, at an interval that's appropriate for the lead.

This logging of activities and setting of new activities needs to be
repeated until the lead is either lost or won.

Appendix 1.2

Example system #2

This system is an overview system that outlines the key steps in the delivery of a web video. It's a great example of how you might break down a very complex system. This is very typical for a service-based business when trying to document the delivery side of their business. Over time, additional subsystems may be developed to support many of the steps listed.

Title: Video product process for videographer

Knowledgeable worker: Adrian

Description: This is the entire video production process for videographers.

Step #1: Client comes onboard
- Client has been <u>onboarded by project manager</u> and paid their deposit, so work can commence.

Step #2: Discovery session
- Project manager organises a date with the videographer for a Discovery Call with client.
- The videographer has a <u>Discovery Call with the client</u> and takes notes/locks in shoot date if possible.
- The videographer advises the client on whether a <u>script or interview would work best.</u>
- The videographer notifies the project manager about any <u>additional equipment required.</u>
- The project manager adds the shoot date into the calendar.

- The videographer condenses and <u>adds their notes to the project management software.</u>
- The videographer <u>fills in the Equipment Calendar</u> with equipment required and pick-up/drop-off dates.

Step #3: Pre-production
- The project manager <u>emails the client with some preparation advice</u> and the Discovery Call notes.
- If concept ideas were requested by the client, the videographer needs to <u>come up with some great ideas.</u>
- The project manager sends the videographer the first draft script or bullet points.
- The videographer <u>revises the script or writes a script from the bullet points provided.</u>
- The videographer <u>creates a storyboard, shot list, outline or brief</u> (if required) and <u>sends to project manager through project management software</u>, who sends it on to the client.
- <u>The day before the shoot</u>, the videographer picks up gear and <u>checks the Gear Checklist.</u>
- The videographer then arranges to <u>buy any hard drives or batteries</u> that are needed for the shoot.

Step #4: Production
- The videographer MUST <u>run through the Shoot Checklist</u> before the shoot and again when they arrive.
- The videographer sets up the camera, thinking about <u>the appropriate visual style.</u>
- The videographer sets up the lights (<u>lighting indoors/lighting outdoors/lighting the face</u>).
- The videographer checks the <u>ISO</u>, <u>shutter speed</u>, <u>aperture</u>, <u>white balance</u>, <u>focus</u>, <u>frame rate</u> and <u>shooting format.</u>

- The videographer reminds themselves on <u>how to get a great performance from their presenter.</u>
- If working with a crew, the videographer reminds themselves <u>how to call the set.</u>
- The client or presenter enters and gets their <u>microphone attached by the videographer.</u>
- The videographer <u>checks the audio levels.</u>
- The videographer informs/reminds the presenter on <u>how to best read from the teleprompter.</u>
- After the shoot, the videographer MUST <u>check the After Shoot Checklist.</u>

Step #5: Post-production

- After the shoot, the videographer MUST <u>backup the footage and audio onto the studio computer.</u>
- The videographer <u>stays organised by duplicating template folders.</u>
- The videographer needs to <u>follow the editing basics,</u> <u>find the best takes</u> and <u>create a narrative edit.</u>
- Once the main structure is complete, the videographer needs to review their hours spent and <u>notify the project manager of their progress.</u>
- The videographer needs to <u>find and place stock music,</u> <u>find and place stock footage</u> and/or appropriate <u>after effects templates</u> to enhance the video.
- The videographer then <u>adds appropriate B-roll</u> that was shot for the video.
- The videographer needs to <u>colour-correct and colour-grade the footage</u> to look natural and pleasing.
- Once the video edit is locked off, the <u>videographer needs to mix and master the audio.</u>
- Once everything is complete for the first draft, the videographer

MUST <u>run through the Edit Checklist</u> to ensure everything has been addressed.

Step #6: Delivery

- The final video(s) must then be <u>exported for the web</u> in the right format/bitrate/codec.
- If encoding a workshop, the videographer must <u>encode at our standard workshop export settings.</u>
- The video(s) are then <u>uploaded to video hosting service</u>, inside a newly created project with the <u>standard naming conventions.</u>
- Then, in project management software, the <u>project manager is tagged in a comment containing any notes and the video hosting service link.</u>
- The project manager <u>sends off the first draft.</u>
- The project manager posts any changes for the second draft into project management software and tags the videographer.
- The videographer makes those changes.
- Then, in project management software, the project manager is <u>tagged in a comment containing any notes and the final Wistia link.</u>
- The client signs off on the final video or pays for extra changes.

Step #7: After the video is complete

- The project manager assigns tasks to clean up video hosting service and to upload the finished video to our YouTube channel.
- The project manager makes a note in the project management task of where the footage is kept (which HD and its location).

APPENDIX 2

[ ] C H R I S   [X] D A V I D

W E E K L Y   A L L O W A N C E   S C O R E   S H E E T
FOR THE WEEK COMMENCING MON 23/05/88

B E D T I M E S

BY...	7.45	8.15	8.45	9.15	9.45	10.00	10.15	10.30	11.00+	Teeth	Pray
Mon	+12	+8	+4	+2	-5	-15	-20	-25	-50	+-2	+3
Tue	+12	+8	+4	+2	-5	-15	-20	-25	-50	+-2	+3
Wed	+12	+8	+4	+2	-5	-15	-20	-25	-50	+-2	+3
Thu	+12	+8	+4	+2	-5	-15	-20	-25	-50	+-2	+3
Fri	+10	+9	+8	+7	+6	+5	+2	-5	-30	+-2	+3
Sat	+10	+9	+8	+7	+6	+5	+2	-5	-30	+-2	+3
Sun	+12	+8	+4	+2	-5	-15	-20	-25	-50	+-2	+3
OUT	.	.	.	.	.	+12	+10	+8	+4	+-2	+3

Bedtimes Total   .....

B E D R O O M
Clothes put away (M) T W T F S S (+4 ea)   .....
Bed Made & Tidy (M) T W T F S S (+4 ea)   .....
Clothes/Books/Toys/Litter on Bedroom Floor (-5/time) .....

K I T C H E N
Lids off containers/Fridge items left out (-7ea)   .....
Dishes/Food left on Breakfast Bar (-5 ea time)   .....
Rinse/Stack all dishes/pots & wipe benches after
        - Lunch   .   .   .   .   S S (+9 ea)   .....
        - Dinner M T W T F S S (+9 ea)   .....

B A T H R O O M
Bath M T W T F S S (+ or -5 ea)   .....
Towels folded on rails M T W T F S S (+2 ea)   .....
Towels left in hall or bedroom (-6)   .....
Excessive water on bathroom floor (-10)   .....

L O U N G E
Food dropped on lounge furniture/floor (-5)   .....
Dishes/food containers left in Lounge/Dining (-7)   .....
Clothes/Books/Toys/Litter left in Lounge/Dining (-5) .....

R U M P U S   R O O M
Cupboard tidy - top 3 shelves (Chris) (+8)   .....
Cupboard tidy - bottom 3 shelves (David) (+8)   .....
Cupboard left untidy more than 3 days (-8)   .....
Dishes/food/clothes left in Rumpus/Family (-7)   .....
Clothes/Books/Toys/Litter in CAVE part of room (-5) .....

G A R A G E / F R O N T   Y A R D
Tools left out of garage (-7)   .....
Boards/bricks/bike at front door or on driveway (-10).....
Anything left in front yard or on nature strip (-5) .....
SUBTOTAL THIS PAGE   ....

1

W E E K L Y   A L L O W A N C E   S C O R E   S H E E T   Contd.

W O O D Y (David only)
Fix Food/water - (M) T W T F S S (+6 or -4 ea) .....
Cage Clean & Greenery - MON WED or SAT (+7ea)   .....
20 mins taming - (M) T W T F S S (+5 ea)   .....
Cage not cleaned all week (-20)   .....

C A T (David only)
Fed on   - (M) T W T F S S (+6 or -4 ea)   .....

F I S H (David only)
Fed on   - (M) T W T F S S (+6 or -4 ea)   ....

R A B B I T / G U I N E A   P I G S   (Chris only)
Given vege scraps   - M T W T F S S (+2 ea) .....
MORNING Hutch Shift   - M T W T F S S (+5 ea) .....
AFTERNOON Hutch Shift   - M T W T F S S (+5 ea) .....
Hutch NOT shifted on   - M T W T F S S (-8 ea) .....
Wash hutch box & fit liner/straw - SAT or SUN (+12)   .....
Hutch box NOT cleaned for more than 2 weeks   (-20)   ....

R E L A T I O N S H I P S
Hurting brother after being told not to   (-2000) .....
Hiding/Concealing/Not telling the truth   (-50)   .....
Hurting brother (with or without reason)   (-25)   .....
Display of temper tantrum   (-25)   .....
Directly disobeying an instruction   (-25)   .....
Answering back/Mocking when spoken to   (-25)   .....
Bad manners at the table   (-15)   .....
Calling someone names he/she does not like   (-10)   .....
Actively Provoking or Continuing a Dispute   (-10)   .....
Waking parents up except in emergency   (-10)   ....

T E L E V I S I O N   A N D   P L A Y   T I M E

NOTE Time shown as PLAY must not include any TV/video viewing!!
     Only PLAY time spent with another person is counted.

	WATCH TV or VIDEO (Up To)								PLAY (Over)		
	None	30min	1hr	90min	2hr	3hr	4hr	5hr+	1hr	2hr	3hr+
Mon	+15	+11	+9	+7	+3	-5	-30	-50	+5	+6	+7
Tue	+15	+11	+9	+7	+3	-5	-30	-50	+5	+6	+7
Wed	+15	+11	+9	+7	+3	-5	-30	-50	+5	+6	+7
Thu	+15	+11	+9	+7	+3	-5	-30	-50	+5	+6	+7
Fri	+20	+15	+12	+10	+9	+7	-5	-50	+5	+6	+7
Sat	+20	+15	+12	+10	+9	+7	-5	-50	+6	+7	+8
Sun	+20	+15	+12	+10	+9	+7	-5	-50	+6	+7	+8

                                   TV and PLAY Total .....

SUBTOTAL THIS PAGE   ....

2

W E E K L Y   A L L O W A N C E   S C O R E   S H E E T   Contd.

G E N E R A L   H O U S E   C A R E
Shoes/Dirty socks away from Bedroom/Front Door   (-5) .....
Clothes/Books/Toys/Litter in Passages/Stairways (-5) .....
Damaging/breaking toys soon after purchase   (-10) .....
Dirty marks/mud on windows/walls/timber deck   (-10) .....
Knock anything into Guitar/Hi Fi speaker box   (-100) ....

B O N U S   P O I N T S - U n d e r   S u p e r v i s i o n
Tidy Up House as directed by Dad (+5 to +10)   .....
Wash windows (+4 ea window)   .....
Hose and wipe garage door (+7)   .....
Wash car (+20)   .....
Vacuum House (+7 ea room)   .....
Help Wash or Dry Dishes (+15)   .....
Clean Fish Pond (+15)   .....
Water all indoor plants - up to 3 times/wk (+8 ea)   .....
Water all recently planted trees in garden (+10)   .....
Burn The Papers - up to 2 times/wk (+10 ea)   .....
Help Get Soap/Towels for Mum/Dad   (+5)   .....
Wash Black Tiles and Timber Deck   (+10)   .....
Wash Tiles in Foyer & 3 Bathrooms   (+15)   .....
Demonstrated good manners all this week (+10)   .....
Special Act Of Kindness (to be described) (+10)   .....
Neatly/Accurately Filled Out Score Sheet (+3)   .....
Reading Exercise Accomplished (David only) (+10)   .....
Other ....

TOTAL BONUS POINTS   ....

O V E R A L L   P O I N T S   T O T A L   ....

S C O R E   L E G E N D
Under 200   NIL
Over 200 points $1.50
Over 250 points $2.50
Over 300 points $3.50
Over 350 points $4.50
Over 375 points $5.50
Over 400 points $6.50
Over 450 points $7.00

Over 200 points for 10 weeks in a row   EXTRA $7.00
Over 300 points for 5 weeks in a row   EXTRA $10.00

Missing target for a week of a sequence can be made up by keeping
target for TWO weeks (to compensate for the one missed).

3

Glossary

Critical Client Flow (CCF): A SYSTEMology tool used to identify the central 7–12 systems used to deliver your central product/service. Download template: www.SYSTEMology.com/resources.

Departments, Responsibilities & Team Chart (DRTC): A SYSTEMology tool used to assign roles and responsibilities and identify knowledgeable workers who will play a key part in the development of systems. Download template: www.SYSTEMology.com/resources.

Department head: A person responsible for overseeing a department.

Knowledgeable worker: A person who has knowledge of how to complete certain tasks within a business to a high standard. They're also the person who is recorded as they complete that task, preparing it for documentation.

Leader: This person is often the business owner. They're great at inspiring others into action. As the business grows, the highest and best use of their time is in setting the strategic direction of the business. They're quick movers, thinkers and problem-solvers.

Manager: This person is the perfect complement to the leader. They're expert at running the operations side of the business. They're detail-oriented and love taking projects through to completion.

Systems champion: The person who takes ownership of the systemisation of a business. This person has a high attention to detail, loves systems and helps to keep the SYSTEMology process moving forward.

Acknowledgements

I COULDN'T HAVE WRITTEN THIS BOOK ALONE and while I mention many mentors, collaborators and friends throughout the book... I wanted to say a special thanks to a specific few.

Carrolyn Jenyns, my wife, my rock, my inspiration.

My boys Nathaniel and Jordan, I will be the best example I can be.

Allan Dib
Brad Sugars
Gino Wickman
Melissa Crowhurst
Michael & Luz Delia Gerber
Mike Rhodes
Nik Thakorlal
Pete Williams
Simon Bowen

Business Systems Summit speakers and guests – too many to mention but you have all played a very important role in getting me to this point. Thank you.

SYSTEMology® team – Bill Doerr, Emma Goff, Eric Putnam, Kristian Basilio – hold onto your hat, we're about to go for the ride of a lifetime.

SYSTEMologists™ and partners – you are the messengers and it's time to take this message worldwide. Thank you for believing in us, and together we will change the world.

Our clients – a few of whom have shared their stories within this book and the hundreds of others who have helped refine my process.

You, the reader – well done on buying this book. Like Neo did in the Matrix, you have just taken the red pill. Welcome to Wonderland; I will now show you how deep this rabbit hole goes.

About the author

David's entrepreneurial journey began in his early twenties when he sold Australia's most beloved sporting venue, the Melbourne Cricket Ground. Since then, his business experience has spanned from franchising retail clothing stores to founding one of Australia's most trusted digital agencies, Melbourne SEO Services.

In 2016, he successfully systemised himself out of that business, hired a CEO and stepped back from the daily operations. Through this process, he became a systems devotee, founding SYSTEMology.

Today, his mission is to free all business owners worldwide from the daily operations of running their business. To achieve this, Jenyns spends most of his time supporting the growing community of certified SYSTEMologists as they help business owners implement SYSTEMology. He also delivers workshops, keynote addresses and hosts his own popular podcast – *Business Processes Simplified*.

Connect with Dave at:
www.SYSTEMology.com

Lightning Source UK Ltd.
Milton Keynes UK
UKHW041011080920
369511UK00003B/93/J

Lightning Source UK Ltd.
Milton Keynes UK
UKHW041011080920
369511UK00003B/93/J